TABLE

PART 1	The start	2
50 Ways to Invest in YOU		
Part 2	Obstacles	69
Part 3	Your Future Depends	103
Part 4	Choices	134
Part 5	Being a GOOD PERSON	169
Part 6	New Experiences	203
Part 7	TIME	235
Part 8	Missing Parts	271
Part 9	Your Future part 2	303
	FINAL THOUGHTS	333

Who Will You Be?

Have you taken any steps to invest in yourself? Recently? Do you know what investing in yourself means or looks like? It is a proactive process. Self-investment requires focus, deliberate action, and regular attention, and when you do so you can reap unimaginable rewards.

This book has been designed to encourage you to think differently about your life and to be more proactive about investing in yourself. You need a framework to understand the basics of personal investment and to understand how best to tackle it. That is what we are here for.

In the poignant words of author and poet Ralph Waldo Emerson – "The only person you are destined to become is the person you decide to be?"

Who will you decide to be?

What It Means to Invest in Yourself

What does it mean? To invest in yourself.

Everyone has their own special gift(s). If they take time to uncover and hone them, then they can share those gifts with the rest of the world. Your gifts are no different. If you take time to uncover those gifts and polish, develop, and grow those gifts, then they will reward you in kind. That is what it means to invest in yourself. It is something you have because you believed in the future enough to invest in your gifts and goals now. Your hope can guide you.

There are all different ways in which you can invest in yourself. It can be as simple as focusing on brushing up on a musical skill or improving your health or learning a brand-new skill altogether. Of course, you can do all those things. The point is that you think about the gifts you have, the skills you would like, and how you can work toward achieving those things. If you put the work in, then the reward will be great.

Self-improvement through investing in yourself does not need to be a grand scheme or gesture. The small changes can have a big impact, especially when those small changes add up. For you, it could be setting aside five minutes daily to practice a new language. It might be something major, like going back to school to pursue a master's degree.

Begin by identifying your portfolio. What does that mean? It's essentially a skills matrix. You are taking stock of your existing skills, the gifts that come to you naturally, and your traits.

Are you good with people? Great with technology? Or better with animals?

Make a list and you have your personal portfolio. You can invest in yourself by determining where to go from there.

It is all about looking at yourself as you are and choosing to believe that you are worth the time and energy to invest more.

Benefits of Self-Investment

- Investing in yourself helps you become who you want to be

- Investing in yourself is investing in the most important person in your life

- When you invest in yourself, you are taking control of your life

- Self-investment allows you to make your dream life your real life

the thoughts you think, the actions you take and the mindset you engage today, will help shape, mold and predict your future.

- With self-investment, the sky is the limit.

- Whatever your dreams may be, achieve them with self-investment.

- Self-investment helps you create the best version of you

- Self-investment is the key to happiness

- Investing in yourself is the key to personal growth and development

- Investing in yourself affirms your belief in yourself

- Investing in yourself affirms your value and self-worth

- Self-investment can transform your entire life

- Self-investment strengthens you and better prepares you for the unexpected

- When you invest in yourself, you create a better future

- Investing in yourself elevates your mentality

- Take control of your life and start investing in yourself today

Preemptive Planning and Action

You invest in the things and people around you. You socialize with your friends, which is a way of investing more in your personal relationships. You spend your time playing a game on your phone or scrolling social media, that is a time investment.

In a lot of social media situations, there is an emotional investment, too. Often, the greatest investment you make is pouring all your time and energy into your job. You are making an investment in your career to the benefit of your employers. It takes time, energy, and even money to build connections and gain recognition to pave the way for career success.

To invest in yourself truly, you must plan and act on the back of those plans.

Invest in Yourself.

When someone starts a business, they start investing in themselves. Not only are they leveraging their existing skills, but they are also putting their total trust in themselves, believing fully in their ability to succeed and they are stretching themselves.

The value that they create on the back of that business is a massive reward and it is one they do not have to share anymore. It is a big step to take, it requires having the utmost confidence in your own skills, strengths, and abilities.

Investing in yourself in any way is just like that. It is an act of trust, a signal that you trust yourself and believe in yourself enough to believe that you can be more than what you currently are. Starting a business requires giving up lots of other interests and activities, at least for a time, because all your energy and focus is poured into the business.

I would encourage you to think about self-investment as a business startup of sorts. Except, in this case, all your time and energy are being poured into learning, developing, growing, and creating more value in your life.

You do not have to sacrifice all your hobbies or all your spare time, but it's important that your focus shifts to value-adding activities to help you get to where you want to go.

There will be times where your sole focus is on self-investment, but self-care is an act of investment. Choose activities, hobbies, and tasks that encourage learning, growth, and the furthering of wisdom and knowledge.

When you make the choice to practice self-investment, you must go all in. What that looks like to you is dependent on where you want to go in life. There are countless ways and countless reasons why you would choose to invest in yourself. Getting a good handle on the reasons why you wish to seek improvement is a good place to start because knowing why will help you figure out the what and the how.

So, what do you want from life?

Do you want to climb the career ladder? Do you want to build your own business? Do you want to deepen your romantic connection with your partner?

Humans are hardwired to want to grow, to do better because this is what has increased the likelihood of survival. It is the reason we find growth and development addictive once we get started. It is a critical aspect of your happiness and progress.

Often, self-improvement and self-investment attempts fail. That could be for many reasons, from being unsure of which direction to walk or not being clear enough on what you want to invest. Let us focus on how to proceed. Goals are important, but there is more to it than that. You cannot stick with should, it is time to embrace must.

Objectives

If you do not have goals in mind, then you will need to consider what you want to accomplish. Picture yourself a year from now, five years, ten years, etc. Identify the end goal and work backward to determine your objectives which will help you create milestones to reach and give you an idea of when you need to reach them.

Purpose

What is your purpose? More importantly, what is the purpose driving your goal? It is easy enough to say I want to climb the career ladder, but it is insignificant if you do not understand the purpose behind the want. Self-improvement is meaningless otherwise.

You need to know the purpose behind your goals because that is what brings fulfillment.

For example, you want to climb the career ladder because you want to earn more money because you have other passions you would like to pursue. Or you want to be a better parent because your childhood was difficult, and you wished you had had stronger parental support.

The purpose will drive you and when you are faced with obstacles or challenges, nothing will deter you from overcoming them.

Life Areas

You can begin planning by assessing different areas of your life.

Your Personal Self

Where do you want to be? Where do you want to go? What do you want to do? How do you want to grow?

Relationships

What relationships require more attention? What work on yourself can help you deepen those bonds?

Health

Your mind and body function better when you are healthy and energized. What investments can you make in yourself today that will support your health in the future?

Finances

Do you have money issues? Are you simply poor with money? Do you have financial goals? Aspirations? Determine what goals you have in this area and plan what you can do today to secure that future.

Now you just must put it all together to create an action plan that works to support those investments.

Other Key Life Areas Include

- Mental and Psychological Health
- Emotional Health
- Professional/Work
- Spiritual Development
- Lifestyle

The key is to think in terms of choices, plans and goals that you develop today, which in turn will boost your tomorrows.

How What You Today Invests in Your Future Self

Your actions, thoughts, habits, and behaviors have a profound impact on your happiness, well-being, and future. The situation you are in now is a result of your past thoughts, behaviors, habits, and actions.

Today, you have the option to make small changes by investing in yourself positively now in order to create a better life for the future you. Let us talk about some of the ways in which you can do this.

Book It

If you want to get started, then put it on your calendar and do it in a way that ensures you cannot wriggle out of it no matter how hard you try. Obligations that you cannot get out of are going to help you make proactive changes for future you.

Sign up for classes, join a community group, book a visit with friends, whatever it takes. Create a calendar that reflects what a social, happy, active person would make and stick to it because guess what? You can be a social, happy, active person!

Retirement Savings

This might sound wild, but your retirement plan should start now. By taking care of it now you are literally investing in your future self. You do not want to work longer than you must just to make enough money to pay the bills and put food on the table.

You have spent a lifetime doing that, take care of that now so you do not need to worry about it when you are not as young and energetic as you once were.

Learn to Cook.

Learn to cook now and not just any cooking, learn how to cook healthily. You can meal prep, plan, or whatever it takes. By learning to cook you are investing in your health, your finances, and your overall happiness and well-being. Of course, cooking can also be an excellent stress management tool.

Time Capsule Wardrobe

This might not sound relevant so bear with me. You wear clothes daily and by building a time capsule wardrobe you invest in clothing of a high-quality that will last you for years to come. Spend your money wisely to dress well, it will make you feel more confident and secure inside. The clothing you wear impacts your career; it impacts your life. It is a chance to showcase your personality in a unique way. Think about that.

Separate Savings Accounts

If you want to save money, then create individual accounts to do it. You need a retirement account, that goes without saying, but what about other things? You need an emergency fund, of course, for rainy day issues.

What about an account for travel? An account for learning? Many banking apps allow you to create separate pots that you can custom name. It removes the money from the fingertips of your main account and lets you save easily.

This is not about depriving yourself of needs, rather it is about making sure you fulfill all your needs now and in the future.

Media Consumption

You probably consume a lot of media. What type of websites do you visit? What type of shows do you watch? It might sound odd, but the content you consume influences your feelings and thoughts. If you watch a lot of tense, anxiety-inducing content then you are likely going to feel tense and anxious. Do yourself a favor and pursue more positive content.

Read

If you want to invest in yourself, then reading is a fantastic way to do it. With plenty of classics available free to listen to on Spotify, to download from the internet, and eBooks available for pennies... there is no excuse! Just make time to read and vary your reading material as much as possible.

Reading more boosts your vocabulary, stimulates imagination, increases knowledge and problem-solving skills, relieves stress, and it is entertaining, too.

What you read now can influence who you become, and it is an investment in your future self.

Keep In Touch

Your close friends and family are important. Your social ties help protect your mental health, they provide you with stress relief, advice, and strong bonds that are important to happiness and well-being. People often lose sight of their friendships as they chase life.

Eventually, as you grow older the people you once relied on are not around anymore because too long has expired between phone calls, visits, or texts. Put the work in to solidify your relationships now and remember it is an investment for both your current and future self.

You should choose your friends wisely. The people you spend time with can heavily influence your behavior, thoughts, and actions. If there are friends (or family members) in your life who negatively influence your behavior, thoughts, and actions, then do what you can to distance yourself from them.

Plan And Measure

You cannot set goals and leave it at that. Once your improvement goals are in place you must act and make it happen. Make your plans and set out to achieve the goals you chose.

You will need to track your progress and measure results as often as possible to ensure you are still on the right track. Self-improvement is a never-ending journey, and you won't get far if you aren't willing to a) monitor yourself and b) constantly invest in yourself.

Sometimes there are shorter paths to take to achieve things. For example, if you want to invest in yourself by learning how to play the piano then you will learn far quicker if you commit to practicing one hour each day, as well as hiring a teacher.

But you can still make some improvement by practicing daily on a piano you purchase for home and using an app. One will, of course, get you where you want to go quicker. If you stop to measure your progress regularly, then you will know when and how you can get there quicker.

Block External Influence

You should worry about approving of your own decisions rather than worrying about what others may think of your choices. Forget what everyone else thinks. If you are being true to your values, beliefs, and priorities, then you are making the right decisions for the person you imagine you will become.

You can greatly influence the course of your life and who you are by making some strategic plans and taking deliberate actions today that will shape and mold your future!

Overview

There are 8 lessons included in this book that discuss 8 key considerations when planning to invest in yourself.

- Lesson #1: Invest In Yourself - Identify What Holds You Back

- Lesson #2: Invest In Yourself - Make A Life Plan

- Lesson #3: Invest In Yourself - The Choices You Make Today Will Shape Your Future

- Lesson #4: Invest In Yourself - Identify Your Values

- Lesson #5: Invest In Yourself - Learn Everything You Can And Broaden Your Horizons

- Lesson #6: Invest In Yourself - Life Is Short, Value Your Time And Spend It Well

- Lesson #7: Invest In Yourself - Surround Yourself With Quality People - Winners, Supporters And Optimists

- Lesson #8: Invest In Yourself - Create A Personal Development Plan

There are also 8 workbooks that accompany the lessons so you can begin to develop plans and analyze your own personal situations.

Introduction

Several people on this earth spend loads of time, and money, investing in other people, or physical possessions, and therefore neglect the person they should be investing in most, which is themselves! Investing in yourself is more important than almost anything else because you are the only person who you will have to spend the rest of your life with.

If you are not sure how to start investing in yourself, it is quite easy, but here are some ways to begin the process.

50 Ways to Invest in Yourself

1. Exercise

Investing in yourself means investing in your health, which starts by engaging in regular exercise. Recent studies have found that sitting behind a desk all day is just as bad for you as smoking, so make sure you try to get at least 30 minutes of exercise at least 5 days a week.

Cardio based exercise which brings your heart rate up (and keeps it there) is best, but make sure you do not overdo the exercise for your level of physicality. Biking, swimming, jogging, running, gardening, and even housework are all forms of exercise.

2. Stretch

According to Harvard Health, stretching is a crucial part of keeping muscles strong, limber, and healthy. Therefore, besides just exercising regularly, you need to stretch regularly as well. This helps keep your joints and muscles flexible and helps lower your chances of an exercise or work-related injury.

Some form of yoga is usually recommended, but even just a few simple stretches at home when you wake up in the morning can go a long way. The experts recommend that you stretch at least once a day for best results.

3. Cook Healthy at Home

Part of investing in yourself also means you need to take the time, and effort, to cook meals at home. Not only is this generally healthier than eating out at a restaurant, but you can control portion sizes and investigate all the ingredients which go into your food.

Some people find it easier to eat healthier when they rid the house of all the junk food, so they are not tempted and fill the fridge with healthy items instead. Make sure your diet is loaded with plenty of fruits, vegetables, and proteins, and skip out on the added salts, fats, and sugars whenever you can.

Challenge yourself to cook something new and look up the recipe for something you have always loved at a restaurant and try making your own version at home. This will help keep cooking, and sticking to your diet, more fun than just eating salads.

4. Pack Healthy Snacks

How many times do you visit the snack vending machine while you are at work? Did you know these items are usually loaded with trans fats and other ingredients which directly affect your health? Start planning and pack healthy snack for yourself from home, such as carrot sticks, almonds, or a healthy fruit and nut bar.

You will likely feel more alert, and your wallet will thank you too. If you have a desk at work, consider getting a few dedicated snacks to leave there too, such as a container of raw almonds, that way you will always have a snack even on the rare occasion you forget to pack one.

5. Skip the Takeout

Whether or not you pack the healthy snacks, you do need to start skipping the takeout. Take-out food, or fast food, is some of the worst food you can put into your body. Even if you select a healthy item from the menu, it is usually packed with unnecessary calories and sugars which probably do not fit in your diet.

If you are the kind of person who is too tired in the evening to cook after a long day, then consider meal prepping healthy meals for the entire week on your day off. Portion them out, and package them individually so that you will have an easy meal waiting for you when you get home.

6. Drink Water

According to WebMD, drinking water is one of the most critical things you can do for your health. Every system in your body relies on water to function, and when you deprive these organs of the water they need, you could be heading down a long road of health problems.

Not only that, but dehydration drastically affects your mood and ability to concentrate. Experts recommend drinking at least 8 glasses of water each day. And skip those sugary or diet beverages as those only end up dehydrating you more.

7. Drink Green Tea

As you are switching out your beverages, consider incorporating more green tea into your diet. In over 15 different studies, people who drank 2 to 6 cups of green tea a day had lower amounts of body fat and generally weighed less than those who did not. This is because green tea's polyphenols have been shown to boost metabolism and speed up the fat burning process.

Green tea has also been shown to lower levels of inflammation, as well as risk factors for certain diseases like heart disease and cancer. Just make sure that when you enjoy your cup of tea, that you stick to unsweetened, or a small amount of honey, and do not add any sugar, as this will counteract all the good benefits you are trying to gain from drinking it.

8. Sleep More

No matter how you look at it, your body needs sleep. The CDC in the United States recommends that all adults from ages 18-60 years should get at least 7 hours of uninterrupted sleep each night. Besides just getting enough sleep, you can improve the quality of your sleep as well. Start by establishing a bedtime and wake up time for yourself, then work on sticking to them.

Make sure you are not drinking any caffeine or sugar near bedtime. Experts also recommend leaving your cellular device, or TV, off and in the other room starting 30 minutes before bedtime.

Also consider investing in a natural wake up alarm which eases you awake instead of jolting awake to a buzzer. You just might find that more, restful, sleep is just what you needed to feel like a new person.

9. Take Care of Your Health

Taking care of your health certainly is not easy, as it involves a combination of all the above to truly make a difference. But, additionally, taking care of your health also means going to a doctor when something does not feel right.

And this only grows more important as you get older. Several conditions, which are caught early on, are easy to cure, but once they can get worse, they could cost you your life. Ensure you stay up to date with routine doctors' visits, and do not hesitate to call when something seems off. Also note that this means seeing a mental health professional as well if you feel yourself struggling with your mental health.

10. Create A Mantra

Like Pumba in The Lion King, you can help yourself get through those tough times in life (which will inevitably arise) by creating your own personal, positive, mantra. This needs to be something which specifically speaks to you. Once you come up with it, any time you start having negative thoughts try blocking them with the mantra. You can also write the mantra on sticky notes and place them around the house for you to see and remember later.

11. Get Up Early

People who get up early in the morning are generally more productive than those who sleep in. Not only that but pushing the snooze button has shown in several studies to make you more tired rather than help you feel more rested.

And this applies on the weekends too, you should be getting up at the same time each day of the week in order to keep your body consistent. And soon enough, getting up early will not be difficult at all.

12. Have A Morning Routine

Wondering what you are going to do in these mornings when you are up early? Well investing in yourself means it is time to have an established morning routine. This can be something simple like brushing your teeth, exercising, and then taking a shower. But if you really want to take yourself to a new level of success this morning routine should also include some time for journaling, meditation, goal setting, and the planning of your day.

13. Journal

Even if you do not have time to do it in your morning routine, keeping a journal is an important part of growing with yourself. You cause this journal to reflect on things which have happened, as well as write and track goals.

At any given time, you should have two lists of goals in your life, those for the short term, and those for the long term, and a journal is a great way at keeping these all-in-one safe places. Either way, try your best to journal at least once a day, but for best results you should journal both in the morning and in the evening in order to check back in with how your day went while it is still fresh on your mind.

14. Plan Your Days

This is another reason to keep a journal. You will stay more focused and on task if every morning you write a to do list for yourself for the day. This goes beyond simple household chores and errands if you really want to take control of your life and invest in yourself you should also plan things such as your phone or social media time. This way you will not be constantly checking your phone or wasting valuable time when it could be better applied somewhere else in your life.

15. Meditate

The benefits of meditation are so vast there is truly no reason you should not be trying to meditate on a weekly basis. Meditation has been shown in numerous studies to reduce stress, control anxiety, and help reduce early memory loss. It also helps the practicing individual become more self-aware and be able to focus for a longer period.

In order to get the best benefits of meditation, it is recommended you find 10 minutes of each day in which to meditate. If you have trouble clearing your mind, you can attend a yoga class and often the instructors there will teach you breathing techniques which can transfer to meditation. For best results, meditate both in the morning and in the evening.

16. Keep Yourself Organized

Staying organized is a favor your current self does for your future self. Because no one wants to go digging for that one thing that they may need for that one project. If you are not already organized, head to your nearest home store and pick up a few tools to help you get situated.

Try to organize everything so that you can find it quickly and easily when the time comes. Labels are a great feature especially when you are dealing with several different bins of supplies!

17. Have Goals

Investing in yourself means having goals. And as previously mentioned, you need to write these goals down on a daily, or at least a weekly basis to keep them fresh in your mind and keep yourself on track. If you do not think you have any goals, it is long past time to make some!

So even if you are not sure where you want to be in a few years, start by making a goal for the month, no matter if it is to save money, or perhaps try a new restaurant in town. The whole point is to set your sights on something, and then follow through and achieve it.

18. Track Your Results

Whatever your goal may be, you need to keep track of your results in order to keep yourself on track. If your goal is a weight loss one, weigh, measure, or take pictures of yourself regularly, and write about how you feel with each step you make.

It is recommended to keep all this information succinct in something like a journal, but social media can also be a useful tool as long as you have a following of people who support you on your way to your goal.

19. Let Go of Things That Anger You

Believe it or not, holding on to and suppressing anger can cause physical damage to your body. It can lead to increased blood pressure, liver damage, and muscle aches, as well as a myriad of other physical symptoms.

Therefore, you need to make a conscious effort to let go of the things that anger you. You can do this during your meditation, your journaling, or by arranging to see a therapist. Regardless of how you decide to learn to let go, the first step is deciding that you will, and the rest should follow more easily.

20. Work on Your Emotional Health

Besides just anger, working on your emotional health is a critical part of investing in yourself. This means, not only are you letting go of negative emotions, but you are also responding to situations differently. You no longer let yourself feel attacked when someone says something against you, instead you handle it with grace.

You also do not engage in childish behaviors like tantrums or physical fighting. If you struggle with this, practice having a mature emotional response, which works for you, before the situations come your way. Learn how to diffuse yourself, and try a few different methods as needed.

A deep breath, or minute to think, can work wonders! Then next time you are faced with a difficult situation, employ this new tactic, and gauge the results. You might be surprised by your own success.

21. Let Yourself Dream

It may seem a bit silly, needing to allow yourself to dream. But dreams are often the precursors to goals. Of course, they need a little editing before you can write them in your journal and start working towards them, but do not let that stop you from having them in the first place!

In fact, if you truly want to achieve your dreams, start analyzing them and asking yourself just how you intend to get there—before you know it, you will be there!

22. Explore Your Creative Side

This goes right along with dreaming, sometimes as humans age they forget to indulge their creative side. Which is sad, because this is the side that helps you overcome obstacles on your way to achieving your dreams.

So next time you have a cute idea, do not suppress it, instead act upon it. And do not let anyone tell you otherwise. And if you are having a hard time getting the creative juices to flow, find something that inspires you, whether that's music, movies, or even reading a book. Whatever your tactic may be, make sure you devote some time to it so the creative part of your mind can truly grow.

23. Spend Time with Friends

Also, as you age, you tend to spend less time with your friends as you all grow older, have children, and begin to lead busy lives. This is unfortunate because research has shown that not having a good group of friends to spend time with can lead to insomnia, digestive problems, diabetes, and even heart disease.

Humans are social creatures who were meant to live in communal environments, and so loneliness can hit hard. Try to try to get together with your friends once a month, even consider making an event out of it like game night.

And even if everyone cannot come every month, leave the invite open and whoever can come, will. If physical hang out are simply impossible, you can also consider starting a group chat or zoom game night while the kids are sleeping.

24. Surround Yourself with Like Minded People

Besides just having friends, you also need to make sure you have the right friends. People change as they age, and as you grow you may find that you do not have anything in common with some of your old friends anymore and that you are simply headed down different paths.

If this happens to you, and you are struggling where to go to meet new friends who share your interests, consider joining a Facebook group or community club for an activity you enjoy. Currently there are Facebook groups for any and every hobby, so you are bound to find a group which meets up for whatever activity keeps you love!

25. Leave Toxic People Behind

This goes right along with maintaining friendships and surrounding yourself with like-minded people. If you find, as you pursue your dreams, that certain people suffer from the victim mentality and are nothing but negative all the time, then it is time to start eliminating them from your life.

This can be tough, especially if the toxic person is a family member, but you can start by resolving to see them less, and only speak to them when necessary. You are the reflection of the people you hang out with, so the last thing you want to do is hang out with someone who has a negative world view and is not investing in themselves.

26. Put Your Phone Down

Do you know how much time you spend on your phone? Probably a lot more time than you think! And generally, unless you are a social media influencer, time spent on your phone is time wasted, and if you spend too much time looking at other people's lives it can start to damage your health.

This does not mean you have to delete social media; it just means you need to establish a certain time of your day to spend on it, then spend the rest of the day doing something else. For example, if you work in an office and eat lunch alone at your desk, maybe this can be your social media time.

Or, if you get home half an hour before your husband or wife does, you can spend time on your phone before they get there. Either way it is time to be more mindful of your phone usage because your phone never invested anything in you.

27. Always Be Polite

As you start to go out and meet new people, or even just as you come across people in your everyday life, it is important to be polite. This is because you never know who may be there when you need a favor.

There are countless stories of interviewers who sit in the waiting room and watch how the interviewees treat the secretary. If they are rude, they are sent home before the interview. Do not let this be you, and instead just strive to be polite to everyone you meet.

28. Find Someone You Look Up To

As you embark on your journey to success by investing in yourself, it is likely you may lose you way or become discouraged at some point in time. Therefore, it is critical to find someone you look up to and remember their story the next time you are discouraged. This way you can ask yourself how your idol would deal with the roadblock and feel inspired rather than discouraged.

29. Always Be Learning Something New

According to scientists, every time you learn a new task or expand on one you already know, your brain makes new neural pathways. And having a brain which is constantly creating these new neural pathways delays the demyelination of your brain, which means it keeps your brain from forgetting things and developing issues like dementia.

In all that time you are no longer spending on social media, pick up a new skill—this could be anything from learning a new language, or trying a new hobby.

And if you find you do not like it halfway through, do not be afraid to try another new thing, and then another. Basically, in order to properly invest in yourself you should always be trying new things.

30. Play Brain Teasers

Similarly, to learning new things, engaging in brain teaser activities daily can help keep your mind functioning longer, and enable you to be independent for more years when you are older.

So, download a few word games on your phone and plan to spend about thirty minutes a day solving them for the best results for your brain. And if you are having trouble finding time for these, perhaps consider replacing most, or all, of your social media time with these brain teasers.

31. Visit New Places

While your mind develops new pathways when learning new things, you also develop new pathways when visiting new places!

Not only is travel good for your brain, but it also lowers stress, and boosts happiness and satisfaction.

Travel also expands your mind and horizons, as you encounter people who are different than yourself and step outside your comfort zone. Even if travel is not possible for you, consider visiting a new part of town, or maybe just a new restaurant you have never been before, anything which will lead you to broaden your current life view.

32. Read 30 Minutes Each Day

Several successful CEOs in the United States report that they read at least one book a week. This is because reading is one of the number one way to invest in yourself and broaden your horizons. Reading a non-fiction book is like receiving a free education and is directly linked to success.

There is a reason unsuccessful people can never finish a book.

So set a goal for yourself—experts recommend 30 minutes a day for best results. But you could also aim to read one book per month, and you will already be ahead of 75% of Americans. Try to stick to nonfiction books, and start with a topic you are interested in. But if you read a few nonfiction books, it is also okay to throw a fiction one in there for fun occasionally too.

33. Create A Vision Board

Another way to keep your creative juices flowing while working towards one of your existing goals is to make a vision board. Grab a cork board from the store and cut out pictures and sayings from magazines which embody your goal.

If arts and crafts are not really your thing you could also do this online with a Pinterest board. However, you may decide to go about it, just make sure you put your vision board somewhere visible that you can reference multiple times a day and remind yourself what you are working towards.

34. Always Look to Improve Your Skills

No one is ever "the best" at anything. You may think you are the best, but even if you think it, there is already someone out there learning to do it better. Therefore, even if you may think you know everything, it is time to have some humility and recognize that you likely do not. Part of investing in yourself is bettering the person you already are.

And in order to do that, you must point out your own weak points. Maybe you are an excellent employee, but bad at following through. Maybe that is something you need to work on. Are you a great listener but lack empathy? This could be something to work on as well.

No matter what skills you may already possess, continue to work on bettering them every day and know that there will always be more to learn.

35. Have a Hobby

How do you spend your free time? Is it doing something which will improve the future you? If all your free time is spent on your phone or watching TV, this is not the case. Instead, it is time to turn off the media and invest in a meaningful hobby.

It does not have to be anything fancy; it could be something you have always wanted to do, like learn to scuba dive, or start a garden. No matter what your interests are, it is time to invest yourself in them, so that you will have something to show for your years later in life rather than a list of all the TV shows you binged on.

36. Find A Way to De-Stress

Several studies run by Harvard Health have found chronic stress to be a major steppingstone to disease and an overall unhealthy life. Experiencing major stresses can impair cognitive function, lower immune response, and even increase the chances you will die from heart disease. It is critical that you find a way that you enjoy destressing and invest in it for your own future health! If you engage in meditation, this should help daily.

But you also should have an activity which helps you de stress in more major ways, such as a weekend getaway, or a trip to the spa for a massage. Whatever your choice de-stressor may be, make sure you make some time in your life for it.

And if you find your stress level is still climbing out of control, it is okay to seek help, or consider cutting out some of your obligations which are not part of your goals.

Even though you may not want to, you will likely find you feel better (and are better prepared to attain your goals) without over stressing yourself and wasting your attention elsewhere.

37. Practice Confidence

While on your self-investment journey, it is also necessary to put some time into building your self-confidence. Besides just creating a mantra, you will want to make over your body language so that other people can see you are self-confident as well. This is also the time if you are used to being pushed around, learn to stand up for yourself.

The reason you are investing in your self-confidence is because it is necessary to have a strong belief in yourself during your journey—in order to keep yourself on track when things may get difficult. If just anyone can talk you down, then you are liable to be completely knocked over mentally at any point.

If you are struggling with bringing up your self-confidence, consider reading a book about it, or even just mentally (and physically) preparing yourself for things more often. This can help you feel more confident when a certain event comes around because you will be prepared to handle it thanks to your previous thinking.

38. Put Money Towards Experiences and Not Things

No matter what you think of possessions, they will never love you back, nor will they ever be invested in your success. And when you buy possessions, often time this is not something which will help you grow mentally.

Rather than acquiring clothes, cars, or shoes, consider investing in an experience which will make you richer as you invest.

This could be anything from a class to learn a new skill, or a trip to see a new locale.

If something like clothes or shoes is really your passion, then consider learning to make these items, or designing your own pieces, as a mental expansion to just simply shopping for them in the store.

39. Get Rid of Clutter

This is closely tied to spending money on experiences, not things. When you buy too many things, chances are they will begin to pile up and become clutter in your life. People with a lot of clutter are often disorganized physically, as well as mentally.

Start getting your life in order by clearing out the clutter and donating, or trashing, the things you do not use. As a rule of thumb, experts say if you haven't used something in a year, you probably don't need it.

40. Improve Your Communication Skills

Communication skills are a critical part of being able to flourish within our society. So, as you embark on your self-investment journey, make sure you work to improve your communication skills. If you do not know where to start, there are several places which offer classes to teach you the art of communication.

You can also do your own research online and then try out your newly learned skills at your next get together. Remember that communication skills includes both verbal, and nonverbal forms of communication, like body language.

41. Create A Budget

Although investing in yourself does not necessarily mean financially, it is still a part of it in the grand scheme of things. You cannot invest in yourself financially when you are overdrawing your checking account each month or using your credit card to make ends meet. Stop this habit by making a budget and sticking to it.

There are several budgeting apps which can help you with this, or you can use the old envelope trick, where you pull out all your money in cash and put it in separate envelopes for what it is supposed to be spent on.

When the envelope is empty, you can spend no more money in that category for the month. If you are having trouble not overspending, consider cancelling things like your TV show subscriptions, or cutting back on the number of times you eat out and eating at home instead.

42. Live Within Your Means

So now you have a budget, and it is time to live within your means. Therefore, no more using credit cards. When your friends invite you for a night out, if you do not have any more money to spend, learn to say no. This is an important step of investing in yourself, as you cannot move forward financially if you are always accruing debt which is pushing you a step back.

Sometimes people find it easier at this step if they physically destroy their credit card by cutting it up. Or you can freeze it in an ice block in the freezer, so then if you needed to use it, you would have to wait for it to melt, giving you time to think if you really need to spend the money on the purchase or not.

43. Have Debt? Get A Side Job

Conceivably, if you have followed the above two steps, you now should no longer be adding new debt to your life. But what if you have debt from before? Now is the time to pencil any amount of money left in your budget toward debt repayment. Consider cutting back on fun spending to pay debt down even quicker—as this will lead to you being debt free much faster.

If your debt is simply massive, in the thousands of dollars, consider getting a side gig like food delivery or dog walking. You might be surprised at what a difference even just $200 extra dollars can make in a month when it goes towards paying off your debt. Before you know it, you will be debt free, and that is the most amazing feeling.

44. Save Money

While you are paying down your debt, it is difficult to save money. And honestly, paying down your debt is more important that saving, at that point, because your debt is likely growing.

Once your debt is trimmed down, or gone, it is time to reroute some of the money you were paying towards debt into savings (you can add back some fun things as well but aim to save 10% of your income if you can).

This will keep you from sliding back down the slippery slope of debt in the future, especially if an unexpected bill comes up. And saving money is literally the financial version of investing in your future self, and you will never regret that you did it.

45. Make the First Move

Sometimes in life you will be discouraged. Maybe you had a job interview, and they did not call you back, or that cute guy or girl did not ask for your number. Life is too short to wonder what might have been. Instead, save your future self-time and needless thoughts by making the first move. Have not heard from a job interview? Call them and ask why.

At least then you will know in future interviews what to do differently. Ask that cute person on a date. Want to try something crazy like bungee jumping? Do not wait for a friend, ask a friend to go with you instead! If everyone on earth was always waiting for someone else to make the first move, nothing would ever get done! Be the change you want to see!

46. Step Outside Your Comfort Zone

This is part of making the first move. In society, we are often told to wait until we are ready, but if you are doing something truly crazy, chances are you will never be ready. Now is the time to step out of your comfort zone and force yourself to do something new, try something different, be the person you always wanted to be! You will never regret it, and this is one of the best ways to invest in the expanding of your horizons.

47. Write A Letter to Your Past and Future Self

Do you wonder just how far self-investment can get you? It is important to track your progress. Do this by writing a letter to your past and future self. In the letter to your past self, forgive yourself for anything you may have done wrong and acknowledge everything you have done to get this far.

Then, write a letter for your future self, and tell yourself everything you want to do, and where you want to be in five years.

Then close them and resolve not to look at them for five years (or longer). If you write a physical letter, this is very easy to accomplish. You can also do this digitally, but then tuck away the letter in a desktop folder which tells you the date to read it.

Likely you will forget about it, but when you do find it in a couple years, it will be amazing to check in with yourself and see all your progress! Hopefully, you will be further than you can even imagine now!

48. Do not Compare Yourself to Others

It is also time to stop comparing yourself to others. No two people on this earth have the same journey or the same dream. You are completely unique, and there is absolutely no reason to compare yourself to others, ever.

If you find you struggle with this, create a second mantra reminding yourself how unique you truly are. And when you look at someone in jealousy, or dismay, repeat your mantra and know you are one of a kind.

49. Forgive Yourself for Mistakes

Whatever you have done in life, no matter how bad it may be, it is forgivable. But before you can move on and become a success, you must forgive yourself for these mistakes. Remembering that you are human, and that everyone makes mistakes, can go a long way.

If there is a physical reminder of a mistake you made, it is time to get rid of it, as this can help free you from emotions such as guilt and regret. And you will likely make more mistakes in the future, and you must know this is okay. Learn from your mistakes, then forget them, and move on so that they do not hold you back from achieving your dreams.

50. Find Happiness Within Yourself

Last, but certainly not least, investing in yourself means you know that you are the only person on this earth who can make yourself happy. Happiness is a perspective, and it is a decision. No matter what is going on in your life, if you decide you are happy, no one can take that from you. Now is the time to make that decision.

Make changes in your life to make it better, and decide that regardless of what comes your way, that you will be happy in everything that you do.

Investing in yourself is not a one-time thing. It is a process, a lifestyle. But once you choose it, you will never look back, and your future will be bright because of it. Even if you cannot do all fifty things on this list, or are overwhelmed by it, consider conquering a handful of them at a time, maybe just five.

And when you conquer those, then try five more. You will be surprised at how easy it is once you get started—so do not delay and start investing in yourself today!

PART 2

Table of Contents

Introduction	72
Identifying Obstacles	73
Understanding Excuses & Limiting Beliefs	73
Working Through Excuses & Limiting Beliefs	75
Negative Meaning	78
Wait & See	79
Test the Water	80
It is Holding You Back	81
Thought Examination	83
Seeking Clarity	83
Habits, Actions, Choices	84
No More Justifications	85
No More Blame	86
Self-Reliance	87
Be Accountable	87
Develop Knowledge	88
Looming Failure	88
Relationships	89
Getting to Grips with Limiting Beliefs	90
The Real and The Imagined	93
Take Back Control	93
The Confidence to See Things Differently	95
Once Upon A Time	96
Deletion	97
Distortion	98
Generalization	98

Mind-Reading	99
Polarization	99
The What Ifs	99

Introduction

Have you ever looked around at your friends and family and wondered how they seem to constantly achieve their goals while you seem to be standing still? There is nothing more frustrating because as much as you want to be happy for them and celebrate their wins, it is difficult not to beat yourself up for being unable to do the same.

You are not alone dealing with this. There is good news, though, because you can invest in yourself to ensure you do achieve your goals, but first, you must identify what holds you back.

You must remember, moving forward, that you are the only person who has the power and control to move forward or to hold you back.

Identifying Obstacles

Understanding Excuses & Limiting Beliefs

Are you guilty of making excuses? It's easy to get caught up in excuse-making when we allow complacency, fear, or insecurity to drive us. They will only ever hold you back.

A limiting belief is generally influenced by a circumstance, situation, or event that left you feeling powerless. Both excuse-making and limiting beliefs can hold you back and hinder you from making progress.

Limiting beliefs are often unconscious, they are there underneath everything driving your actions, thoughts, and words. They are quietly shaping your reality and they are creating the gap between what you say you want and what you do.

I want you to think about that for a moment. Imagine that deep in your unconscious mind there is a set of instructions or values embedded. This set of instructions is what will determine the thoughts that you think, the words that you speak, and the actions you follow-up with. Your experiences and the situations that you have lived through created that unconscious set of instructions. You created that programming, you embedded it, even if it was unconscious.

If you have had overwhelmingly positive experiences throughout your life, then you are being empowered by a positive set of instructions. However, if you have been through a lot of trauma, experienced a lot of negativity, or had a difficult life, then there is a good chance those experiences have tarnished your set of instructions and may be creating a negative view of the world as a result. That is where limiting beliefs come from.

In some cases, it is easy to spot patterns of limiting beliefs, negative excuses, and emotions because they pervade your every thought and conversation. But sometimes they can be challenging to pinpoint because in those cases we layer the excuse in some form of truth. It makes it difficult to argue against those excuses because there is evidence to hold up as truth.

Working Through Excuses & Limiting Beliefs

What do you want? Why don't you have it? What is stopping you? That should help uncover some of the limiting beliefs and negative emotions hiding beneath layers of excuses, whether there is truth in it or not.

You can work through some of these excuses and limiting beliefs by journaling about specific areas of your life where you experience the most frustration or where you feel as though things have stalled. Then, you must gain awareness of when a negative voice chimes in to tell you that you are not good enough or that you do not deserve to have it all. Pay attention to when those feelings crop up and write about them.

When was the first time in your life you started to experience those types of feelings? How old were you when they first arose? There is every chance it was somewhere between three and eleven years old because those years are known as the imprint period. The point at which your experiences in childhood have the most impact on who you will become, how you feel, how you behave, and how you will represent yourself later in life.

This is an important stage of childhood and children must be empowered to understand their emotions and feelings during this time. If they are not given the opportunity to do so, then there is every chance that child will struggle to achieve their potential as they grow up.

When you look back on those feelings and determine when they began, you must ask what happened, who was present for it, how you felt, and see how that negative belief or excuse grew from the experience. You need to understand how it affected you at the time, how it limited you thereafter, and how it continues to hold you back now.

You might not have learned anything from the circumstance, situation, or event at the time. However, it is not too late to take the lesson forward with you. When you look back on key moments you can change it from a negative experience to an empowering, positive one. You can replace that limiting belief, negative thought, or statement with one that empowers and motivates instead. It is making a commitment to challenging old beliefs to spark your true desire.

Negative Meaning

The negative voice that speaks to you quietly, telling you that you cannot, should not, will not, or are not good enough, is something most people hear from time to time. The problem is when you listen to it you make excuses for the voice and when you make excuses for it you effectively accept what it is saying as truth. You might not realize it, but it is an act of giving up.

You must challenge those assumptions and you have to look at the stories that you built around untrue things. Assign a new story to the situation and make it an empowering one. Let us look at the ways you hold yourself back by layering excuses in truth.

Wait & See

When a new opportunity rolls around, there is an excitement. When it feels right it is thrilling because you can recognize that it makes logical sense. Yet, there is a voice in the back of your head, and it is whispering to hold off, it might even be screaming for you to think on it longer. There is no harm in a wait and see approach, is there?

It sounds like the mature thing to do, but the reason you feel its right is that you fear what may come next. That fear is filtered through your limiting beliefs and negative emotions. It is not logical, it is fear. When you continue to wait and see you set yourself up for failure because you start failing to recognize the many opportunities that come your way.

If opportunity knocks you must be ready to take the call. You must be strong enough to evaluate the pros, as well as the cons. If you get to the end of the process and all that remains is fear, then you must act appropriately.

You cannot sit around waiting for the perfect moment because the perfect moment does not exist (unless you make it yourself), it won't come, and you will be waiting forever.

Test the Water

Can you think of something you desperately wanted, but instead of going after it, you decided the safest bet would be to dip your toes in just to test the water first? Living in this gray area will only lead to conflict and confusion. But how much you put into things matters, the universe will respond in kind. You will only get out what you put in in any given situation. Are you making a positive contribution to your life?

An obstacle is a milestone, it is an opportunity to endeavor beyond to overcome. You would not run into any obstacles if you were not making progress. So, when you run headfirst into a challenge or an obstacle, remember it is only natural to run into resistance when you're making strides. Enough of this dipping your toes in, you are either in or you're out.

It is Holding You Back

What do you think is holding you back? You probably spend a lot of time thinking about what you want from life. How often do you think about why you have not yet achieved what you want from life?

You want a promotion, but what have you done to make it happen? What is standing in your way? Perhaps the company offers no room for growth, or there is no opportunity for you to move up the ladder. Maybe it is worse, maybe your boss doesn't recognize the value you offer and keeps overlooking you when promotions roll around. Perhaps you struggle with co-worker cooperation and people make things difficult for you.

Whatever those obstacles are, I want you to understand this – in most cases, the obstacles that stand between you and what you want, the problem is you. You know what you want and when asked to determine why you're not there you seized on a multitude of excuses.

If there is no room to grow at your company, then you could have moved onto another company. If your boss doesn't recognize your value, then you make sure they do, or you move onto another company. If you struggle with your co-workers, you sit down and come up with a plan to ensure their cooperation. Or you move on.

There is always a choice and by erecting these barriers and holding onto them, you are choosing to fall at the first hurdle. Let us work on eliminating what holds you back.

Thought Examination

How you think about opportunities (and yourself) directly align with your results. If you believe in your abilities, skills, and yourself, then you will be able to create results. When your negative thoughts are so deeply embedded that you are not aware of negativity, they will always derail your efforts. You must make a conscious decision to examine your thoughts and correct the negative ones that crop up. Replace the old one with a new, positive one, and retrain yourself until you root it out.

Seeking Clarity

If there is anything that will weaken your progress quickly, it's a lack of clarity. If you know what you want and it's something different from the life you lead now, you won't get anywhere without first finding clarity. You're stifling your progress.

If you invest in yourself by allocating contemplation time to seek clarity, then you invest in your future. This is a great place to start if you are confused or frustrated about what you want. Create a safe environment or habit that allows you to fully clear your mind to seek clarity. Make it a habit.

Habits, Actions, Choices

The habits you allow to take root result in your actions and choices. It might not be consciously, but it is what brings about the results you have thus far. If you want to shift the results you are experiencing, then you must begin by changing your habits to positively influence your actions and choices. Once you have spent time seeking clarity with your thoughts you can bring those habits into your realm of awareness.

No More Justifications

Stop making excuses, stop finding a way to justify the position you are in. While there is nothing wrong with trying to better yourself, it is important to understand that by constantly making excuses and justifying your position you are knocking yourself out of the game.

You explain it away by saying it will take too long, it is just too difficult, I am not clever enough, no one understands, it doesn't feel safe to change, everyone is struggling now so it's not time to rock the boat. It is all justification. It is all excuses.

You are just going in circles and arguing with yourself and it is getting you nowhere. While your head wants to keep you safe and your justifications sound logical and intelligent, you are only holding yourself back.

No More Blame

Unless you are prepared to be fully accountable for your results you will always fall back into the blame game. When you blame others (whether it is people, circumstances, or situations) you paint yourself as a victim.

When you cast yourself in the role of a victim you are only playing yourself because you convince yourself that positive results are impossible to attain. When you lay blame, you tell yourself that you had no control over the result. You're suggesting that you had no say in the way your life has evolved. Someone else should have taken care of the results you wanted, not you.

By eliminating blame from the equation, you remove the lurking negative shadows that loom over your thoughts and feelings. When you embrace accountability, you become more aware of the many opportunities in your life.

Self-Reliance

When you know what your goals are you must think about what it will take for you to achieve those goals. Then you have to rely on yourself to get the job done. It is not just taking accountability and responsibility for your results, it's also about adopting a positive attitude to encourage success. For every goal you set, you should consider what you need, what skills you have, and who will support you on your path.

Be Accountable

Accountability and responsibility walk together. The more clarity you gain around your results the easier it is to take accountability for your progress. Without it, it is easy to justify when you veer off track. When you do that you simply prolong the journey, and it takes longer to achieve your goals.

Develop Knowledge

Often, people suggest that there is just one thing standing between your current position and where you would like to be and that's learning something new. Knowledge and education are valuable tools and something you should consider if you want to move forward in your life. Your school days may be long over, but education does not cease just because you graduate. Look at each of your goals and consider what learning or education you may need in order to achieve your desired results. Plug that knowledge gap!

Looming Failure

One of the most powerful emotions humans deal with is fear. It can be an overwhelming force, so consuming that it can feel like you are drowning under the weight of it. That fear, whether it's of failure, pain, or humiliation, can interrupt any momentum you have built, and it can shut you down and shut you out from any further progress. Where there is a fear of failure, pain, and humiliation, there can be no forward momentum.

Fear impacts everyone differently. If yours can expand it may intensify and if it can intensity, then you may struggle to ever break free.

Relationships

Ultimately, you will either live up to the standards of the people you spend most of your time with. Or you will stoop down to their standards. What type of standards do the people around you have?

Think about the standards at work, the standards in your relationship, those of your family, and at home. While it is important that you set your own standards, it is just as important that you evaluate the standards of those around you because those may be negative influences contributing to your inability to progress. Do not keep negative influences around just because you are worried about letting go of an old friend.

Remember, your relationships influence your habits, actions, and beliefs and that is one of the first places to start your self-improvement journey, especially when you want to identify what holds you back to properly invest in yourself.

Getting to Grips with Limiting Beliefs

Let us circle back to those limiting beliefs because that is going to be the biggest obstacle for you to overcome. I would like to begin with a story. Tammy received difficult news a few months ago. It was the type of news that shook her to her core.

The foundations that she had relied upon her entire life began to crumble. She was angry. She was upset. She was scared. She started to create stories in her mind to try and make sense of it all. She looked at the challenges and possibilities from her past experiences and she tried to make them make sense. Her experiences shaped how she viewed obstacles and opportunities after that.

Challenges are rarely flexible. You must spend time listening, coaching, supporting, and growing in performance and confidence. Sometimes you will deal with people who are high performing at work and hopeless when it comes to their personal life (and vice versa). Sometimes people get muddled up and lose their path. That is what happened to Tammy. One difficult situation was enough to shake up her entire world and it caused her to question everything.

She was lost. She lost sight of her abilities, traits, and strengths, and allowed the situation to consume her and stall any progress she had made. The stories she told herself, those made-up stories she used to try and explain things, stole her momentum, and started holding her back.

When Tammy faced up to the challenging situation, she had to draw from all the resources within her to make sense of what was happening. The toughest thing she faced was separating the made-up stories that hindered her progress from the factual stories that could help. Not all made-up stories are equal.

Are you dealing with challenges of your own? What stories have you been telling yourself? How might they be holding you back? Let us get to work overcoming those limiting beliefs. It is time to take control back and start investing in yourself to move forward.

The Real and The Imagined

You must look back on the stories to understand the emotions behind them. There is this invisible barrier that holds all your hopes, emotions, experiences, and fears and you have to step through it to determine which stories are real and helpful, made up and helpful, or made up and harmful. By doing this you can gain clarity into your mindset and get a clearer view of the fears that have been driving you (and your decisions).

Take Back Control

When you are caught up trying to make sense of a confusing situation (or world, for that matter), it can be incredibly challenging to remain strong. However, the times when you feel at your strongest as generally the times when you feel the most in control.

You feel in control when you believe that you have a) a choice and b) the influence to determine what comes next. There is a choice when you are faced with challenges and you can choose to take back control.

The human brain craves completion. Control is the main thrust between achieving your potential and altering your behavior. You always need to believe that the choices lie in your hands because only you can activate the choice.

When you do so it triggers motivation and suddenly, you feel a sense of achievement which automatically makes you feel as though you are in control. You have completed something, and it sets off a chain of events to stimulate the brain's pleasure chemistry. It might not sound much, but it is a small way to take back control and change those stories you have been telling yourself.

As much as the human brain craves completion, it bemoans uncertainty, especially when facing unexpected bad news, change, or challenges. When you have a good idea about what happens next your brain naturally calms and can think through the worst-case scenario realistically. Which, of course, makes it much easier to plan what comes next.

The Confidence to See Things Differently

When you are faced with difficult news, challenging situations, or trouble, I would encourage you to ask yourself some questions before you lose confidence and control of what is happening.

- What control do you have in this situation?

- What can you do about this?

- Where can you seek additional information?

- Who can you turn to for support and guidance?

- What will you need from the people around you?

- What lies outside of your control?

From there, you can make a list of your concerns and fears, as well as recording the facts and opportunities. You will know what can do, what you need, and who will be by your side. When you have it all on paper you will immediately feel as though you are in control. The key to taking control of any situation is to be brave and believe in yourself. Perfection does not exist, you cannot make comparisons, you must stick to the facts.

Once Upon a Time

We touched on our propensity for telling stories. What's key is understanding that those stories are obstacles holding you back.

Let us address your limiting beliefs by reviewing the most common limiting beliefs that people struggle with.

Deletion

Deletion is our habit of only paying attention to certain aspects of our experiences while excluding others. For example, imagine yourself looking for your friend in a crowded room. There is noise everywhere, but you focus in on the voice of the person you are searching for. You dismiss the other voices and the background noise to home in on that voice. We do that with the stories we tell, too. We delete information to focus on a specific piece we decide is more important.

The more intact your story remains the easier it is to ensure it will not hold you back. While deletion is sometimes necessary to retain the important things, it is just as important that you do not let go of what will help you while holding on to what hinders you.

Distortion

You choose how you view something, but unfortunately, it can be an incorrect view. For example, when you go for a hike in the mountains you might panic when you see what you think is a bear, but as you get closer you realize it is someone bundled up for cold weather. You might see parts of your story that are simply inaccurate.

Generalization

We are often guilty of drawing conclusions and that is usually on the back of one or two things. I am terrible at giving presentations because the audience always looks bored when I am speaking. We generalize based on our perception of a single event and then we call it a personal truth. By using language like all and always, never, and none, or every we set ourselves up for these unhelpful generalizations.

Mind-Reading

I am a good judge of character. Maybe you are. I can read body language like a profiler. Perhaps you can. We often convince ourselves that we know exactly what someone else is thinking. We think we can recognize their motivations and intentions, the meaning of what they are saying, and how they are feeling. There is no specific information to suggest any of it, we just convince ourselves we are capable of reading minds.

Polarization

The all or nothing thinking where we seize on the absolute worst will happen or the absolute best will happen. Life is not black and white; you have to leave room for plenty of shades of gray.

Emotionalizing

When faced with a difficult situation or challenge it is normal to experience a range of emotions. But when we do experience those emotions, we use them as evidence. Know this – your emotions and feelings are a natural response, and they are always valid. However, your emotions and feelings are not always accurate.

You are entitled to them, but you cannot believe them to be true. Well, I feel these emotions so they must be true. Your emotions can be a result of several things. Like, when you are standing at the front of a room giving a presentation and you glance at the audience and see serious faces or people distracted by their phones. It is easy to feel embarrassed and convince yourself that no one is listening or that you give poor presentations. That does not mean it's true.

The What Ifs

You're standing at the crossroads. You can see your biggest challenge looming large, written on a sign in front of you. As you read the challenge you notice the arrows pointing down different roads, the arrows pointing to the many what-ifs that are unfolding.

They may be what-ifs that lead to better outcomes, perhaps they are what-ifs that lead to worse outcomes. The more you think about the what-if the more what ifs pop up. Suddenly, you are faced with so many different arrows and roads that you do not know what to do.

That is all what-ifs do for you. Remove the what-ifs and focus on the realistic choices that you have, relieve your pressure, and battle the stress.

You are the hero in your story, reader, and the outcome of your life is entirely in your hands. If you want to invest in yourself and chase success, then you must identify what holds you back. Think about that as you choose what stories to tell yourself and believe. It is within your power to rewrite it where necessary. It is within your power.

PART
3

Table of Contents

Your Future Depends on The Steps You Take Right Now	1
What Self-Investment Means	2
Emotional	2
Mental	3
Lifestyle	3
Health	3
Tips For Self-Investment	5
Creativity	5
Self-Confidence	5
Knowledge	6
Health	6
Finances	6
Relationships	7
Play Hard	8

A Bucket List	8
Visualization	8
Take a Time Out	9
Build Life Experiences	9
Know Your Path	9
Read	10
Future-Proof	10
Mentor	10
Insurance	11
Streams Of Income	11
Limits	11
Exercise	12
Sharpen Your Skillset	12
Branch Out	13
Self-Development	13
Final Thoughts	14

Your Future Depends On The Steps You Take Right Now

To become a musician, one must spend countless hours practicing their instrument, studying music theory, performing in front of a crowd, working on chord progressions, and experimenting with techniques and writing. It will require tens of thousands of hours of practice and commitment. It will not just happen because they want it to happen.

It required dedication, effort, and hard work. I spend an hour a day playing the piano and have been playing since I was eight years old. I am nowhere near as proficient as I could be. The real greats spend hours of their day honing their craft. They wanted it. I just enjoy it as a hobby, a hobby I happen to have dedicated a lot of time and effort to.

An athlete does the same. They focus on eating a healthy diet, they work on exercising their body daily, and they focus on their sport of choice, whether it is baseball, football, soccer, or track and field. While they might not realize what they are doing at the time, they have from a young age realized that to get what they want they must invest in themselves.

If you want your life to go a certain way, you must have a plan.

What you are capable of in the future will depend on the steps you take right now to improve yourself. Right now, the two biggest tools in your arsenal are your time and energy. If you direct those then you can be anything you want to be.

What Self-Investment Means

The most basic way to boil down the idea of investing in yourself is to call it the ultimate example of self-love. If you do it right, then it will turn into your most profitable investment. Often, we fall into the trap of self-sabotage.

We continue doing what we have always done, and we convince ourselves that everything will improve eventually. It is wishful thinking. No improvement will come without work, it will not just automatically happen because you think it should be so. You must work at it. You must have a plan that details both short- and long-term goals.

There are a variety of opinions and definitions when it comes to self-investment. But let us use finances as an example. When you invest in stocks and shares you are putting your money where your mouth is and staking a claim to something you expect to reap great returns further down the line. That is what self-investment is.

You are staking a claim on a better future, but it is not money you are wagering. It is your time and energy to seeking knowledge, adding to your toolkit, and improving yourself in meaningful ways to guide your life to where you want to be.

You can invest in many areas of your life and before we talk about the concrete ways in which you can do so, let us first address the areas of your life where you can make progress.

Emotional

If you struggle with your emotions and feel a lot of negativity quite a lot of the time, then this would suggest a need for emotional investment. You must take an active role in emotional management to change the state of your emotions.

Anxiety and depression are, of course, chemical imbalances, however, there are plenty of ways you can help stave them off or at the very least manage any symptoms you experience regularly. If you do not have a diagnosed mental health disorder, then managing your emotions can simply be used to improve your mood and help you manage stress.

Meditation is one of the most effective ways to get to grips with your emotions. It is not just a great calming activity; it is also an effective way to process your emotions.

Mental

With knowledge can come great power, or wisdom, or whatever it is you are trying to achieve by furthering your knowledge. It is far easier to succeed if you have taken the time to learn. People talk about self-development and self-improvement and to achieve a level of mastery over whatever it is, requires you to seek out knowledge.

Understand, knowledge is not always related to academia. The knowledge that you choose to pursue might be related to information about bettering your life. The point is that you should support yourself mentally by pursuing knowledge at every opportunity.

Lifestyle

Your lifestyle should reach a certain standard and it is something that you should work on constantly. If there is an area of your life that does not reach a certain standard, then you will need to take steps to improve it. Only you can determine which lifestyle is right for you to live. Only you can ensure that you have the necessary resources to support that lifestyle. Only you can ensure that the lifestyle you create is one that you enjoy.

Health

Health encompasses both diet and fitness. You can be healthy but lack strength or endurance. You can be strong and mighty but lack good health. You must invest in your health and fitness. You can do that by investing in your body, through exercise, hydration, a good diet, and sleep. All of that, of course, will feed into your fitness levels. But you can zero in on specific fitness goals that support your overall lifestyle and goals.

No one is exempt from self-improvement; it is just that many people choose to opt-out. That is to their own detriment. When you improve yourself, when you invest in yourself, you are not just impacting your self-worth and confidence.

You are also making yourself far more valuable to the people around you. If you are bold enough to improve yourself, you will pave the path to amazing results.

Tips for Self-Investment

By this point, you might have a good idea of what areas of your life you would like to invest in. Let us review some of the most common areas for self-investment and the ones that may benefit you the most.

Creativity

Your creativity has a lot of sway throughout your life. Creativity is what inspires you to have fun, it sparks your innovative side, and it is possible for it to change your life for the positive. If you think back to when you were a small child, if you can remember it clearly, you could entertain yourself for hours.

It did not matter if you were alone, your imagination was enough to build a world and play in it. Your creative mind was your company. It tends to change as you get older, but that does not mean you have to allow your creativity to diminish. It is just that it often gets stamped out of us because most people do not view it as practical, but it's an important part of you.

You can set time aside to work on your creativity, whether it is 30 minutes to paint as you will, an hour to write, or 15 minutes to focus on creating business ideas. You can even spend time brainstorming areas of your life to improve and how you can do it.

Or, how to improve your relationships. Creativity is not just for artists. It is for everyone. You just must find out what puts you in your most creative mood, fuel it and make time for it. If you get your greatest ideas while hiking through the woods, then set time aside to do that.

Self-Confidence

If you want to go places, then you need to have great confidence in yourself! It is what determines whether you have the courage to stand up for yourself when you need to. It will determine whether you are strong enough to walk away from dysfunctional relationships.

It is what determines whether you act on the business plan you carefully crafted. It is going to be the determining factor as to whether you succeed in this life or not.

It is vital that you take time to invest in your self-confidence. Learn to build courage and learn to stand up and speak your truth. The more you believe in yourself, the more self-love that you have, the more value you offer the world, the more you will grow in self-confidence. This is the type of self-investment that inspires the people around you.

Knowledge

The more time you take to learn the more you learn and that is when you realize just how much more there is to learn in this world. It is important that you educate yourself. It should not stop just because you walk away with a degree.

There is still a lot to uncover, about history, the world, and people. Do not just educate yourself on your interests, expand knowledge into a variety of areas. Having as much knowledge as possible is empowering and it also helps you move forward in life.

Make time to invest in knowledge. Choose a subject to focus on and go for it before you move onto another subject. You can gain knowledge through videos, podcasts, books, and articles. There are so many free resources to draw from. And they encompass a wide variety of subjects in which to build your knowledge.

Health

You might work harder than anyone else you know, but it will not mean a single thing if you die before you get the chance to enjoy the fruits of your labor. Therefore, it is vital that you look after your health to ensure that your investments have time to flourish.

You grow older with every passing day and the choices you make each day will make or break your health. You must eat well, exercise often, hydrate, and sleep. This is an investment in your health and by proxy, an investment in your future. By looking after your health, you are ensuring that you have the energy and mental fortitude to tackle whatever other self-investment plans you have. It is key to personal gain.

Finances

It is true that money will not buy you happiness, it's also true that the love of it is the root of evil. That being said, money does make the world go-'round and we all have bills to pay, and we want to play too. Financial independence provides a level of freedom that we all want to achieve. So, addressing your finances is an important part of self-investment. While money does not buy happiness, having the money that provides you the freedom to chase what you want does bring with it a measure of happiness and fulfillment. That simply cannot be argued.

If you want to build wealth, then you can do so by taking small steps. You will have to change your lifestyle, and it might require a transformation of your money habits. Take 5-10 minutes daily to look at building your financial savvy and skills.

Take a long look at your finances and where you often overspend and know you make unnecessary purchases. You can still enjoy the lifestyle that you want without stopping for coffee and a bagel every day.

You can invest in your finances by investing in your cooking skills to avoid ordering in four nights a week. It just takes a bit of creativity; it is a good thing you are already working on that!

Relationships

If you are looking for instant results in your life, then you may want to begin your self-investment journey with your relationships. That might sound like you are investing in others as opposed to investing in yourself, but that is not the case at all.

When you invest in your relationships you are creating strong bonds, you are establishing trust, and creating a support system that will be behind you through the darkest times. This is not a business transaction; it is the very basis of humanity.

We are social creatures by nature. We seek out a community. Relationships take time to establish and even longer to build strong, but they add value to who you are as a person.

Right now, you likely have existing strong relationships, so pouring more into those will yield faster results. However, it should not end there. It is important that you build new relationships.

The results from building your relationships will last a lifetime, which is why I would consider it as an instant result. It may take time to pay off in more meaningful ways but deepening your bonds with people will provide you with an immediate mood boost and dip in your stress levels.

Having said that, you must be mindful of the friends that you make and surround yourself with. You should be investing in relationships with positive, successful friends who are willing to chase their dreams.

They are the ones who are going to help you continue to push to get what you want. Your social group absolutely influences how you interact with other people. If you feel low, uninspired, or negative, look at the people you spend the most time with. What influence have they had on your mood?

Who is around when you feel at your best? Pour yourself into strengthening those bonds.

Play Hard

Think of playtime as self-care. It is difficult to find fulfillment in life when you do not chase playtime just as hard as you chase the work. You will not find results if you're all work and no play.

There is a balance to be found and making time for recreation is an investment in your mental health and overall happiness and well-being. How you play is entirely up to you. However, it should be doing things you enjoy, making time to laugh, and chasing whatever makes you lose track of time.

A Bucket List

Have you ever sat down to create a bucket list? Have you ever thought about the things you would love to do and try before you die? We all have dreams and passions, but how many of us try to write a list and tick it off?

Do not wait until you hit retirement age to get started, start now! By starting the process now, you are making time to figure out to achieve the more challenging things on your list. For example, perhaps you want to visit every natural wonder of the world. Traveling is costly, so you should have time to put a plan together as to how you will make that dream a reality.

Visualization

Visualization is an incredibly effective way to invest in yourself. It is the practice of imagining yourself far into the future to create the ideal life and version of yourself. It is your opportunity to let your imagination run wild. You cannot just visualize it and expect it to happen. You must trace that dream back to where you are now and plot your path. What will it take to get there? What steps will need to be made to achieve that visualization? Then as you take those steps that visualization moves closer to becoming a reality.

If visualization does not sound like it is for you, there is always meditation which we touched on earlier. It has a wide range of benefits.

Take a Time Out

It is easy to get caught up in the idea that you should constantly do stuff. Self-improvement requires action; therefore, action must be constant. That is not the case. Just like it is important to make time to play, it's just as important to take a total time out. You need personal time that involves nothing but relaxation to achieve a state of calm and inner peace. Time outs help you rebalance your mind and find calm in a chaotic world.

Build Life Experiences

Routine is important, but life experiences are just as important. You must build healthy habits and create routines that will keep you grounded, balanced, and in touch with your desires. Likewise, you must make time to experience your desires.

Self-investment means creating some of those life experiences. Why not do something you wouldn't normally consider? Think about new ways to dive outside your comfort zone and break out of the box you have been living in. Fuel life experiences with moments you will always remember.

Know Your Path

Right now, you know exactly where you are in this life. You should be able to point your finger to the areas of your life where you feel deeply satisfied, mildly satisfied, or downright uncomfortable. That is where the self-investment journey begins and ends.

It starts right here with you. It is up to you to decide what steps to take to improve the areas of your life in the most disrepair. What do you want to improve? What challenges do you want to undertake and overcome? It might be emotional, but you cannot practice self-investment without having a good idea of the path you want to follow.

Read

We already touched on the importance of gaining knowledge, but there is something to be said for reading for pleasure as well. Some people might shame you for a profound interest in romance novels, but any reading you do sparks your imagination, helps you develop your creativity, widens your vocabulary, and its stress-relieving, too.

Reading transports, you to new worlds, it makes you think of things differently, put yourself in someone else's shoes, view the world from a different perspective. It is all a wonderful exercise in empathy.

Future-Proof

Generally, when people talk about futureproofing it is for technology. It works for your life too. You do not have to wait until you are 50 to consider your retirement, you can start saving now. You do not have to wait until you reach retirement to consider investing, that is something you can look into now.

Your future might be years away, but the planning starts right now.

When you visualize that lifestyle of your future self, how do you imagine your finances will fall into place to make that happen? That is up to you to start dealing with right now and by making financial investments in yourself right now, you are securing your financial freedom in the future.

Mentor

Do not underestimate the power of a great mentor. Just because you are focused on self-investment does not mean that you must walk that path alone. A mentor or coach can walk alongside you, whether it is part of the way or for years to come.

This is someone who will help you find your way when you stray from the path you have set. It is the person who will pick you up, dust you off, and motivate you when you feel discouraged.

We all need an advocate, and a mentor can be that person for you. That is certainly a steep investment, but it is for you. Speaking of assistance on your path to success, you might want to enlist a financial planner as well.

Insurance

We do not know what is around the corner. It is impossible to predict when a broken leg will have us sitting on the sidelines for a couple of months or a car accident puts us out of the game for even longer.

Sadly, we are all one accident away from total ruin. Insurance is for everyone. You should invest in yourself by investing in health insurance, home insurance, accident insurance, and life insurance. Peace of mind is an important piece of the future pie you are putting the ingredients together for. Anything can happen, but you can put plans in place now to protect your future regardless.

Streams of Income

If you lost your job tomorrow what would you do? Start considering how you can create multiple streams of income. The economy is not stable enough to ignore. There are so many people working multiple jobs because that is the world we live in.

One job cannot pay the bills. Creating multiple streams of income helps you secure financial stability, which leaves you plenty of wiggle room if something goes wrong. Think about how the investments you have made in yourself can help you create additional streams of income.

Limits

Everyone has limits, but if you don't know what yours are it will make it really easy for other people to cross them. Learning how to say no to people is just as important as being able to say yes to opportunities. What are your limits? Where have you drawn your boundaries? Do you know when to say yes and when to say no? Know your limits, draw your boundaries, and stick to it. There is no point investing in yourself just to waste all your time and energy on meeting other people's expectations and needs. Part of getting to grips with your limits and boundaries is getting a better understanding of your strengths and weaknesses. It makes it easy to figure out where to push and when to pull.

Exercise

We already touched on exercise a bit when we discussed health, but it is important enough for its own section. Exercise is an excellent form of self-investment. With regular exercise comes stress relief, a boost in energy, better brainpower, improved memory, and more creativity. It can help keep anxiety and depression at bay, as well as protecting against lifestyle diseases.

Just because you should exercise daily does not mean you have to spend money to do so. You do not have to run out and join a gym. You can do it without equipment in your house or yard, but you can make small investments in weights or other equipment you know you will make use of. There is also a litany of free apps you can follow for easy at-home, equipment-less exercises to focus on any area of your body you wish.

When you build your life plan, you had best include plenty of time to get regular exercise. It might sound annoying, but it is important. The key to ensuring you are consistent in your workouts is to choose a regimen you genuinely enjoy.

If you hate jogging do not focus on jogging! If you loathe early morning runs do not go running in the early morning. If you enjoy biking then take every opportunity to hop on the bike, whether it is on the road or stationery.

Sharpen Your Skillset

Do you want to invest in yourself? You must strengthen the skills you already possess. Think of your strongest skills, the ones you rely on the most, and ask yourself whether you are an expert. One of the easiest and most efficient ways to invest in yourself is to build on the foundation you have already built. It is easier to become an expert in what you already know than to start fresh.

If you plan to remain in your current industry or you are on the right path and trying to sharpen up, then you should aim to become the best at what you do. You should look at the skills to determine what is most useful and focus on those first. If you plan to jump to another industry or path, then strengthen the most useful skills for that change.

Branch Out

As important as it is to strengthen your current skill set, it's equally as important to branch out by developing new skills. You are never too old to grow and learning new skills will keep your mind sharp and it gives you more in your arsenal.

Consider what new skills would help you succeed in your industry or the industry you plan to shift to. Focus on those skills first. If you to move up the ladder, focus on learning management techniques. If you plan to start a business in addition to your current job, then focus on time management skills.

Self-Development

Self-development is not necessarily the same as self-improvement or self-investment. Self-development can help you on your way to creating a better life for yourself. What it does do is feed into the necessity of creating a life plan.

The purpose of self-development is that you explore ideas, books, concepts, courses, or whatever that will allow you to imagine your life as you desire it to unfold and determine how to develop in order to get there.

Self-development is figuring out where you want to go, what it will take to get there, and breaking it down into milestones to chase until you reach the top. Likewise, it is important to set goals on your self-improvement journey too.

Final Thoughts

One of life's biggest rules to live by is to invest in yourself. If you are not willing to invest in yourself who else will invest in you? It is up to you to act and it is you that needs to take responsibility and be proactive.

You must be yourself, but you must take steps to ensure that you are the best person possible. Invest in yourself physically, financially, emotionally, spiritually, mentally, and watch as the future you unfold in front of your very eyes.

Take everything you learned above and put it together in a life plan that serves you. Your future depends entirely on your ability to invest in yourself.

It is time to take action, otherwise, you'll be left behind.

PART

4

Table of Contents

Introduction	138
Small Choices Can Have Big Results	139
The Elements of Choice	144
Examples of Specific Choices Made Today That Can Affect Your Future	147
The Reality of Choice	150
Create the Destiny You Desire	150
Self-Belief	151
Self-Discipline	151
Present Living	152
The Right Choice	153
Seek Support	153
Take Risks	154
Never Give Up	154
Self-Acceptance	156
Positivity	156

Gratitude	158
Role Model	159
Hold onto Your Integrity	159
Let Go	160
Focus on Your Locus of Control	160
Assess Values and Beliefs	161
Know Your Value	162
Action	163
Making Better Choices	163
Keen Awareness	163
Careful Examination	163
Visualizing Your Future Self	164
Big Picture Thinking	165
The Wisdom of Hindsight	166
Final Thoughts	168

Introduction

Within you, you hold all the power you need to change your life. The way you harness that power is through the choices that you make. The opportunities you find, the blessings you make, it all boils down to the choices that you make right now. You can change your life, you can change the lives of the people around you, and you have the power to choose your fate.

The choices you make might not seem that deep, but the reality of the matter is that they have long-reaching effects.

For example, and I do not want you to beat yourself up if you enjoy junk food from time to time, but when you stand in front of the fridge deciding what to make for dinner, you have a choice to make. You could save time and effort by throwing a frozen pizza in the oven. Or you could put a little bit of effort in and make a healthy, balanced meal.

How does that one simple decision have long-term effects? Your health matters. The unhealthier dietary choices you make, the more likely you are to experience negative health consequences.

That one choice is small, but it is likely to take you over your daily calorie count. There is a good chance it will negatively impact your sleep that evening, which will leave you tired and stressed out the following day.

It does not stop there. You will struggle throughout the entire day. You will not just yawn through the day, you will be more likely to reach for caffeinated, sugary, high-fat snacks and meals to provide you with the fuel and energy your body needs to make it through.

Small Choices Can Have Big Results

One, small choice... big consequences. That is what I mean when I tell you your choices do not just affect you today. They affect tomorrow. They affect your future choices. They affect your abilities and opportunities, too.

When you feel out of control, whatever the situation, you are likely to withdraw from everyone and everything. You do it to avoid your problems. It is an escape. You escape from those challenges, but by escaping them, rather than confronting and overcoming, then you only prolong them. Your choice is doing you no favors.

The degree to which you withdraw to escape your problems impairs your ability to face up to the challenge you deal with now. More importantly, it impairs your ability to deal with future challenges and obstacles. Life does not get easier, even with an increase in wisdom and a growth in confidence. It is always a challenge. It is always difficult.

That is the nature of life. As we evolve as people life grows more complex because the choices, we make have more stakes. One choice serves as the foundation and more choices build on top of that choice. As this unfolds your ability to handle difficult situations increases. By avoiding choices, you add to your overwhelming.

It is not enough to just make great choices; you must recognize just how powerful those choices are. Your choices impact your life now and they impact your future. Those choices can also have an impact on the lives of others.

Moreover, the choices that you make help shape your thoughts, habits, and actions. Your actions are then interpreted by the people around you after they receive them. They shape the feelings and opinions they hold about you. It alters their perception of you. The perception that others have of you can have a massive impact on your future.

Let us break it down with an example or two.

You must make choices regarding your financial well-being. You make the best decisions you possibly can, but if you have a partner and family then those decisions also impact them. If you make good financial decisions, then you ensure your family is provided for beyond their basic needs. If you make poor financial decisions, then you put their needs at risk just as you do your own.

You must make choices that involve your values. The choices that you make should always align with your values, which is why it is so important that you have a good handle on what your values are.

You cannot make decisions that align with your core beliefs if you have no idea what those beliefs and values are. Those values are your guiding light and if your choices stray from them, you will go nowhere fast. Certainly, nowhere you want to be.

You make choices every day as to how you treat the people around you, whether it is your spouse, children, parents, co-workers, or the barista at your local coffee shop. That shades their view of you. But everyone who sees how you treat others builds an opinion of you.

The person you bump into when you are running late, and you do not apologize because you are in a hurry and then you arrive at your meeting with a new client and that person is staring back at you. Every choice matters. It is not always easy to see the influence of your choices, though some are obvious and immediate.

It is you who controls your thoughts and actions and in turn, it is you who controls your choices. You must decide how to act and think, even if circumstances feel as though they are outside of your control.

You can't control everything, there are constantly external factors that try to get the best of you. You can't control those, but you can control you and how you react to those factors and circumstances.

The Elements of Choice

It comes down to these elements and when one of these elements' changes, then the rest follow. How you think influences your actions. How you act influences your feelings. How you feel influences your well-being. To get a better idea of how this idea works, we should look at it in action.

You have made a choice regarding your physical well-being. You set a goal to get into better shape. That is not specific enough, so you narrow your goal to running a mile without having to stop to catch your breath. It is a great starting point for your fitness journey. You feel exhausted all the time, both physically and emotionally.

So, you are taking action to change that and by focusing on your fitness you are choosing the most effective way to do so. By taking the first steps to reach a greater goal you spark your motivation and start to think more positively. This in and of itself will ensure you feel better emotionally. The physicality will come as you pursue your fitness goal.

The point is, you make a proactive choice about what you think and what you will do. That had an immediate impact on your emotional state. Proper action begets positive thoughts begets motivation begets the change you want to see.

On the other hand, there are the people who struggle to get motivated. They want to make changes, but they don't know where to start. They work hard to convince themselves to exercise.

Have you ever been in that position? If so, the only way to counteract it is to break it down into smaller steps. If it is too overwhelming, then you have not broken it down enough. You must make one choice at a time. You choose to get up off the couch.

You choose to change out of your clothes into workout gear. You choose to stretch before you exercise. You choose the first exercise and so on and so forth. Do that every time and you are making a series of small but powerful choices. When marathon runners set off to tackle the 26.2 miles in front of them... they start with a single step.

If you want to improve yourself, change your life, and positively impact your future, it starts with a single step. Just one decision at a time.

What is your destiny?

It is your choice to make to ensure that it unfolds. It's in your power you simply have to start being mindful about the decisions that you make and start making positive choices to shape your future.

The sum of your choices is the life you create for yourself, whether those choices are conscious or not. The reality is, you can control the choices you make you simply have to take control of every area of your life and engender self-awareness.

Examples of Specific Choices Made Today That Can Affect Your Future

- The choice to go to college or not can predict the jobs you can get in your lifetime and how much money you will make.

- The choice to eat healthy and exercise will affect your health in old age.

- The people you choose to surround yourself with can affect who you will be, the things you will do and your mindset in life.

- Planning for or not considering your goals and what your life will be in 5, 10 or 15 years are more choices that will shape your future.

- Leaving life to chance is another choice that can greatly impact your future, versus deliberate and proactive action.

- Choosing to be a dishonest person will affect your future relationships, career success, social health and more.

- Choosing to ignore your personal issues, such as unresolved childhood trauma or other deep-rooted pain can affect all areas of your life, including personal and professional.

- Retirement planning involves key decisions that will affect your future.

- The mindset you choose to adopt is a huge consideration that can influence your future. For example, optimists and positive thinkers enjoy better physical health, may live longer, enjoy personal wellbeing, and generally live more successful lives (source: Mayo Clinic).

- Choosing who you marry has great implications on your future and can affect your personal and financial wellbeing.

- The choice to be self-reliant can open many doors that will positively shape your future.

- The choice to live a life that yours, not one dictated by someone else, such as your parents or other authorities is a huge choice that will influence all areas of your life.

There are many more examples, too long a list to count.

The test when you are faced with a decision is to consider: how will this affect my tomorrows?

The Reality of Choice

Just about everything offers you a choice. Every moment of your day includes choices. It is a truth, equally, it is a difficult lesson to learn because it highlights just how powerful we truly are.

The power you hold is not over others, it is not over external circumstances, it is over you. So, start making decisions to your benefit. Start making choices that positively influence your future. Make choices to shape your future the way you have always visualized it.

Create the Destiny You Desire

The one choice you cannot make is when you depart this earth. What you do choose is how you decide to live it. You have to dream big; you have to find your purpose, pursue your passion, and commit yourself to achieve it. You must create the destiny that you truly desire and then make the choices necessary to ensure it unfolds before you.

Self-Belief

It is necessary to trust your gut. Your instincts, attuned to your values, can guide you to make the right decisions. You need to acknowledge your strengths and believe in your ability to do what it takes to get to where you want to go. You are strong enough, good enough, and you are smart enough. No one should be able to tell you any different.

Self-Discipline

You will not taste success until you do the hard work to earn success. That, my friend, requires effort and it requires self-discipline. If anyone understands this concept, it is athletes. They understand the level of choice involved in becoming the best of the best and they must constantly make those choices to support the dream they are following.

It takes commitment to the right diet, to the long hours of work they put into their bodies, honing their craft. Serena Williams won a Grand Slam tennis tournament while she was pregnant. She got to where she is because of her self-discipline. When you set goals, you need to set them high, you must be prepared to stretch yourself and make successful choices to support them.

Present Living

There is not a single thing that you can do to change the past. That is history. Nor can you get yourself stressed out thinking about the future because it has not arrived. You can, however, shape your future and to do so you must live in the present.

By focusing on what you can control, concentrating your energy on making good choices, you are taking small steps to shape the future you want to see for yourself.

The Right Choice

Whatever happens, know this – when you choose to do the right thing it will always be the right thing. The hardest question is determining what the right thing is because it is not always the easiest choice. It certainly is not always the painless choice.

But a good way to figure out if you are making the right choice is to answer two big questions. Does the choice you plan to make compromise your integrity? Are you using good judgment and common sense in making this decision?

Seek Support

You will find success much easier if you are prepared to seek support. Even the world's most successful people know that it is important to seek support from others. Sometimes there will be a gap in your knowledge or a skillset you lack. That is where others can step in to help you where you need to go.

Take Risks

Do not take every risk, take calculated risks. With every risk you take, you accept that there is a chance that you will fail. But, with every failure comes a lesson. You either take a risk and succeed. Or you fail, learn a lesson, and try again.

Ultimately, if you are not failing in life, then you are not growing. If you are not taking risks, then you are not learning. And, if you are not taking risks, then you are experiencing a sort of failure anyway so why avoid failure by failing? It is just failing in your comfort zone instead of failing outside it.

Never Give Up

Life is temporary and so is your position in it. Where you are right now is fleeting, but where you end up... that is all down to you. It's difficult to keep going when it feels as though everything and everyone is against you. It is easy to feel as though that is the case, especially when dealing with obstacle after obstacle.

Ask yourself whether that is real. Is everyone really out to get you? Is everything truly against you? As much as it feels like it, you need to understand that it is your primal negative brain whispering nonsense in your ear.

Every feeling that you experience is valid. Every emotion that runs through you as a response to what you are going through… it is valid. As valid as those feelings and emotions are you must remember that validity does not equate with truth. Just because you feel it does not mean that it is fact. You can acknowledge your feelings and emotions without letting them run roughshod over you.

What you need is persistent determination. A never say die attitude. Never give up, friend. You can do it.

Self-Acceptance

There is nothing more exhausting than pretending to be someone you are not. When you wear a mask and act like someone else it wears you down. Why would you want to be anyone other than who you truly are? It does not matter what other people think.

It does not matter what other people choose. You must choose you. If you are not willing to choose yourself, who do you think will do it for you?

You must practice self-acceptance. The only way to truly invest in yourself and make choices that will shape your future is to start by believing in yourself.

Positivity

I know that people are tired of hearing they should be more positive, but it is true. A little positivity can go a long way. That does not mean you have to be happy all the time or positive every second of the day.

It just means that when you slip into a negative mindset or you feel a negative thought pattern taking hold, you correct it. Often, these negative thought patterns are mindsets are false. They are built on nothing but lies based on the incorrect stories we have been telling ourselves.

You cannot lead a positive life if you are harboring a negative attitude. Even when you are faced with difficult times, you should take a moment to remember that every day you wake up is a gift. It is a fresh opportunity.

Life is far too short to live it any other way. You certainly would not want your nearest and dearest to wake up feeling miserable and live that existence on a daily basis, would you? Why would you want to continue in that vein?

You can write out positive affirmations, you can meditate, you can keep a gratitude journal, whatever it takes to inject positivity into your life.

Gratitude

There is something special about learning to practice gratitude. It might be a bit difficult initially, but as you get into the swing of things you start to see how much more you have than you realized.

When you treat life as the gift it is, it is not difficult to see all the incredible people you have by your side. It is not hard to find the silver lining in even the darkest rain cloud. It gets easier to enjoy the bright spots. It becomes second nature to search for all the blessings.

Role Model

You cannot control other people. You cannot control the choices that they make. You cannot control the way they choose to live their lives. You cannot take control of the values they ascribe to, the beliefs they hold, the thoughts they think, or the actions that they take.

You can, however, influence them. How? The best way to influence others to make good choices is by being a role model and making good choices. Live your values, make choices that align with them, and live positively. The rest will fall into place.

Hold onto Your Integrity

Think about how you lead your life right now. Now imagine that someone started speaking ill of you. Would others believe it? Live your life with integrity so that no matter how terrible someone speaks of you, the people who know you would never believe a word of it. Do not leave room for people to question your values. Make grounded decisions and stick to your beliefs.

Let Go

What is it that is holding you back? You must be prepared to let it all go. When you let it go you free yourself to embrace the good things waiting for you. You can hold onto positivity while letting go of the rest. You must have faith in yourself to make your way forward.

Focus on Your Locus of Control

There is no point getting caught up with the things that you cannot control. There is no purpose in trying to control people, external circumstances, or outside factors. Right now, all you can do is focus on your locus of control. You can only concentrate on what you can do and what that comes down to are your actions and attitudes. Focus on that, it is the only way to shape your future.

Assess Values and Beliefs

I discussed values and beliefs an awful lot. Now is a good time for you to sit down and assess yours. You should think about what is most important to you in this life. You should think about what you believe in and why you believe in it. Often, we carry values and beliefs with us that do not truly belong to us.

At some point in our lives, we picked them up from parents, teachers, youth pastors, pastors, siblings, relatives, and other authority figures in our lives. It is the type of thing that someone said to you once and at that moment, it resonated, and you held onto it. But, at some point it stopped resonating with you, yet you still held onto it.

Your values and beliefs can change throughout your life. They shift and evolve with you as you grow, develop, and improve as a person. Invest time into figuring out which values and beliefs you have unconsciously carried with you despite moving on from them a long time ago. Let go of those old values and beliefs and get in tune with the ones that truly matter to you.

Know Your Value

You do not have to prove your worth to anyone, especially if they have an inability to recognize it. You know your worth and you can prove it to yourself with the choices that you make. It is only you who you need to prove your value to.

No one else matters. When you look back on your life, you should be able to say that you were always yourself, that you always believed in yourself, and that you never wasted a second trying to be a person you are not. You should be able to see that you embraced your worthiness. That you never settled for a single thing less than you deserved.

Action

Procrastination will get you nowhere fast, you have to be prepared to take action! Be eager, be passionate, push your productivity, chase success, and go after what you want. That all begins with the choices that you make today.

Making Better Choices

Keen Awareness

So much of the time we live life on autopilot. We do all the things we do, and we do it unconsciously. If you want to start making better decisions, then you must stop and be aware of what is going on around you. Think before you act.

Careful Examination

It might sound silly, but sometimes a list of pros and cons can help you decide in a pinch. It is easy to over-analyze a situation and get yourself stuck. A list of pros and cons can be drawn up quickly and it can guide you to the most important points related to a decision.

You are standing in front of the fridge again and before you reach for that frozen pizza you run through the pros and cons. It takes seconds to do and at the end, you leave that frozen pizza where it is, it will have its day eventually but tonight you have time to make a healthy dinner.

Visualizing Your Future Self

When you are making decisions that contribute to the shaping of your future, then you should think about your future self. The decision you are about to make... would your future self be happy with it?

Your future self will not be happy that you chose pizza over a healthy meal. Your current you will enjoy it, you will get that instant satisfaction you were looking for, but you are contributing to a poor diet and negatively impacting your physical health.

Big Picture Thinking

You will make multiple choices throughout your day. You make a choice now. If you are being realistic, you know there will be another decision to make, another one similar or entirely different. Life is filled with choices and you must factor in the big picture.

What is the long-term outlook for the choice you are about to make? What is the long-term outlook for several choices like the one you are about to make? Think about how you will feel about it later. Think about the potential consequences.

If you consistently make unhealthy choices, then you are shaping a future for lifestyle diseases and misery. If you consistently make decisions based on your ego, then you are shaping a future filling with meaningless relationships. If you consistently make decisions that prioritize your career, then you may end up in a job you do not like because you chose to chase money.

Does any of that sound like a life you want to live?

That is the difference between making choices as they come up and consciously making choices with the big picture in mind.

The Wisdom of Hindsight

Hindsight is 20/20. If you want to make better decisions to shape the future that you want to live, then use the benefit of hindsight to drive those decisions. We are all human, we all make errors, we all experience failure, and make mistakes.

But the key to bouncing back from those errors, failures, and mistakes is learning lessons to ensure you do not repeat them.

The lessons you learned from the past can help you shape your future because those lessons can help you make wiser decisions than you could make before.

Life is a funny old thing. When we taste failure, it can feel as though it is the worst possible thing that could happen. It hurts. It stings. It is humiliating. It should not be humiliating because you are not the only person to ever fail, and you will not be the last.

The beauty of experiencing failure is not just the many lessons you learn; it is that in order to fail you first must put yourself out there and take risks. You will not get anywhere in life if you are not prepared to take risks.

You could embrace doom and gloom every time you fail or, you could recognize that you only failed because you had the courage to take a risk to push yourself beyond your comfort zone.

To recap. Failure is a good thing if you learn a lesson and hindsight is 20/20. Use both to your advantage to invest in your future self by making positive decisions today that shape it exactly as you have always pictured it.

Final Thoughts

Not every choice you make will lead you to untold success because not every choice you make is as big as that. However, every choice you make opens the door wider to the future you have imagined for yourself.

With every good choice, the door creaks open a little bit wider. Keep making great choices and watch the door fly open to welcome you into the future that you want.

Your choices feed your future, but how it shapes up is absolutely in your hands. So, what choices are you going to make today to make sure that your future unfolds as you have been picturing it?

PART 5

Table of Contents

I Just Want to Be A Good Person	171
You Live by Your Values	173
The Disconnect	176
You Are Your Values	180
Why Some Values Are More Positive	185
Evidence Versus Emotion	186
Constructive Versus Destructive	187
Controllable Versus Uncontrollable	189
Find Yourself	190
What I Believe A Meaningful, Successful Life Looks Like	191
From That Life I Imagined, What Is It That Appeals to Me? What Is It That I Want?	192
Defining Your Values	197
A Guide To Living Your Values	201

I want to be a good person. What does that mean?

That all depends on your specific definition of good. And, if you were to describe to me what your definition of good is it might differ from mine, whether slightly or wildly. The reason for this is that good reflects your values.

If someone values their family above all else, then their idea of being a good person will revolve around building that family and spending time with them. If someone values money over everything else, then their idea of being a good person might be building their wealth. The point is that we all see things differently because our experiences shape us and determine the values, we hold dear.

It is impossible to have a conversation about self-improvement and self-investment without first discussing values. You cannot just hope to grow or aim to be a better person. You must first define for yourself what growth looks like and what it means to be a better person. How do you personally define a good or better person? Getting to the bottom of that will help you determine the direction in which you wish to grow. If you don't do that first... well, you're in trouble.

Unfortunately, a lot of people do not realize just how important their values are, overall or to the self-improvement process. A lot of people instead focus obsessively on feeling good or finding happiness. What they fail to recognize is feeling good will not mean a thing if their values are not in order. If your biggest value is using a swirly straw to drink through a bottle of wine every night, then you will feel better temporarily and make your life worse as a result.

The wrong values mean you are living the wrong life. I am not here to tell you which values good or which values are bad. I am not here to tell you which values will work for you and which values will not. By doing that I might unconsciously try to push my personal values onto you.

That is the opposite of what should be happening here. You need to get honest with yourself to determine your values. It is not just about what values are, but it's about how you find out what your values are, why they're important to you, and what the consequences are for ignoring them.

If you want to live the right life for you, then you need to know your values. It is as simple as that.

You Live by Your Values

Whether you realize it or not, you constantly make decisions from moment to moment every single day of your life. You choose how to spend your time, what to put in your mouth, what comes out of your mouth, what you should pay attention to, where your energy will go, and even the thoughts that run through your mind. You also make a conscious decision to read this lesson.

There are countless other things you could be doing with your time, but you chose to focus on this. Maybe you'll be interrupted thirty seconds from now when your phone chirps with a notification, maybe you'll decide you need something to drink and stop reading to wander to the kitchen.

When distractions arise, you make a simple decision laden in values. You decide that notification is of more importance than the information in this lesson. You choose to prioritize a beverage instead.

Your values are reflected constantly by the way you behave.

This is important because it is easy to say you think this and value that, but we often fail to back that up through our actions.

I can tell you until my face turns blue that I am passionate about climate change, but if you see me driving around town in a Hummer it is not going to have any impact on your climate change opinions.

I can swear down dead that social media is killing us, but if I only use social media to put that message out and I constantly scroll my newsfeed and update my accounts constantly, my actions are telling an entirely different story.

I can tell you that I value honesty, but if I tell lies than I am hypocrite.

You believe you want that job, but when it comes right down to it you have never felt more relieved about no one getting back to you.

You tell your partner you miss them desperately and can't wait to see them, but you choose dinner with your friends instead of dinner with them.

Your actions do not tell lies.

The Disconnect

A lot of people are guilty of stating values to cover up their true values. We worry about others judging our actual values and make up those that sound far greater or more purposeful. It sounds innocent enough, but by doing this it becomes a way to avoid rather than face up to who we are. You lose yourself by chasing an idealized version of you that you are not even sure you want to become.

To put it another way, you lie to yourself because you do not feel comfortable with some of your values and therefore, you dislike parts of yourself. There is a disconnect between reality and self-perception and that's often when trouble knocks on your door.

Your values are essentially an extension of who you are. They define you. When something great happens to a thing or person that you value, you feel good about it. Like, when the team you follow wins the championship, or your dad finally retires, or your partner gets a promotion. Even though they did not happen to you, the fact that these positive things happened to people or things you valued, they feel great for you too.

The opposite can also be true. It feels good when something bad happens to things or people you do not value. For example, many British people threw parties and celebrated with champagne when Margaret Thatcher died.

It may have seemed extreme to others, but these are people who lived through her terrible policies. If there is a rival team that loses a big game, it feels good even though it has no impact on your life. It might seem evil or immoral to someone else, but for many, those are moral victories to celebrate.

So, when you are disconnected from your values…

Like, you claim to value hard work and ambition, but you spend your days off playing video games online. There is a disconnect between those emotions and your actions. The only way to bridge that gap is to change or to remain delusion about the world/yourself.

In the examples above you can see values and devalues in action. The same can be true of yourself. You can value yourself, but you can also devalue yourself. And, if you start to hate yourself with the same intensity as others hated Margaret Thatcher, then you may just be prepared to celebrate your self-destruction. Therefore, people who do not fall into self-loathing cannot understand those who do. It is the insidious idea that there is some part of self-sabotage and self-destruction that feels good, even if it is only in the darkest way. The person wallowing in self-loathing believes they deserve it when awful things happen to them because they feel morally inferior. They believe it is a form of punishment. Karmic retribution. An ugly part of them seeks out the destruction in a bid to justify any misery they feel.

We had massive self-esteem movements during the 70s and 80s and those were all about leaving self-loathing behind to instead embrace self-loving. People who truly love themselves do not gain any satisfaction from sabotaging themselves.

They get their satisfaction from practicing self-care, investing in themselves, and living their values. That is what I want for you. Self-love is so important, but it is not enough on its own. But by practicing self-love and rooting yourself in your values, you make it much easier to love others too.

You Are Your Values

Eat, Pray, Love ignited a trend of women taking off to retreats all over the world to find themselves. The idea certainly was not new. It is something that has been happening for decades. That middle-class person who got a great job after getting a decent education and reaches mid-life and starts to panic about what their life has become. They take off for a week, a month, even a year, cutting off contact with the outside world to try and find themselves.

Whether you have had the experience yourself, know someone, or just wished you could afford such an escape... I think we can all relate. At least, you should because what they are really talking about, what they are chasing is their values. They have realized that something is not right, that something does not fit, and want to find new values or a new identity, which stems from values anyway.

For the people who can afford to run away to do so, this is how the situation unfolds.

They feel under pressure in their daily life. They are under large amounts of stress. Due to that, they feel as though they have lost control over their lives or the direction of their lives. They feel as though they do not know why they do the things they do or even know what they are doing at all. They start to feel like their decisions do not matter or that their desires do not count.

They start to think they would rather learn how to play the theremin and drink margaritas of an evening, but they cannot do that because the demands of work/family/romance/family, etc. are just too great. There is an obstacle to them fueling their desires.

So, they feel as though they have lost themselves. They feel they are no longer navigating. They are just being blown around the sea, directionless and out of control. So, the idea behind an escape is to remove themselves from the stress and pressure to recover and find themselves.

It is about gaining a sense of control back because once the stress and pressure are removed from the equation, they can call the daily shots without worrying about everything or everyone else.

That sounds good, doesn't it? By separating yourself from the force of daily life you also have an opportunity to gain perspective on the way life has been unfolding. You can look at your life and ask whether that is truly who you are, if that is what you care about, if this way of living aligns with what you know of yourself. You see things that require change. You realize there are things you believe in and forgot to think about. You recognize that there are things you do that do not positively contribute to your life. You start to build a new you. The new you aren't really new at all, it's simply you getting back in touch with who you are to construct the true you.

When it comes time to return to civilization and live those values you must be ready. It does not matter where you go through the process, though! You can do it on an island, in the bed of your truck looking at the stars, in your bedroom, office, or at the dining room table. You do not have to escape to a fancy retreat to adjust your values. All you need is perspective.

Your values are fundamental to your identity. You define yourself by what you choose to classify as important. You define yourself by what you prioritize. When money matters above all, then money will define you. If you feel like crap about yourself and you constantly put yourself down because you do not believe you deserve success or love, then that will define you as you are. Your words, decisions, and actions are what define you and those words, decisions, and actions stem from what you value.

Any time you decide to change yourself what you are doing is reconfiguring your values. When you experience tragedy, it is devastating. Not just because you feel hurt and sad, but also because you lost something of value. When you lose enough things or people you value, you start to value life itself. Whether it is after a string of breakups or your spouse died suddenly.

Either way, that was a person and a relationship you valued and now both are gone. It is crushing. And it makes you question everything about life, about who you are, about your own value, and about what you understand about the world. It creates the storm of an existential crisis and you no longer know what to think, feel, do, or believe.

This does not just happen after traumatic experiences. It is also true after positive events. There is not just the joy of achievement, there is a question of what comes next.

Why Some Values Are More Positive

I told you I wouldn't tell you which values bad or which ones were good, but I would still like to highlight why some values are most positive than others. How I plan to do that is by highlight what makes a value a good value. Because what is a good value for you might not be a good value for me and vice versa.

A good value is...

- Constructive
- Evidence-based
- Controllable

A bad value is...

- Destructive
- Emotion-based
- Uncontrollable

So, when you are reviewing values you should use those points as guidance to determine whether it is good for you or not.

Evidence Versus Emotion

Your emotions are valid. They are a natural response to the situations you experience. While they are valid and natural, they are not always factual. Your emotions are not rooted in truth. They are simply a reaction. If you heavily rely on your emotions, you are trusting in an unreliable source and it can be damaging. A lot of us rely on emotions far more than we realize.

We often make decisions and take actions based on our emotions rather than based on information, facts, or knowledge. In doing so, we center ourselves and often trade long-term benefits in exchange for short-term gain.

When you are caught up in this cycle you are effectively stuck on a treadmill where you need more constantly. The only way to jump off the treadmill is to consider the facts rather than your feelings.

Constructive Versus Destructive

This should not be too difficult to discern. The things you value should not harm you nor should they harm others. The things you value should enhance you, your life, and benefit others. The complicated part is understanding what spurs you to growth and what harms you. For example, you can take MDMA and claim it is improving your emotional growth.

You could make that argument stick. But you should not need to take a drug to improve your emotional growth and by doing so you are actively harming your body. Likewise, you can work hard at the gym to improve your body, but if you overdo it and become obsessive about it, it can harm you. Sex can be great for building your confidence, but if you embrace casual sex to avoid relationships and intimacy it's harming you.

Unfortunately, the line between harm and growth can be blurry at times. Sometimes it is not about the value itself, but the reason why you value that value. For example, if you value karate because you like to hurt others with it, it is a bad value.

However, if you value karate because you want to practice self-defense, it's a good value. It's the exact same exercise, but the value is different. Sometimes, values are all about intentions and those intentions will determine whether a value falls into constructive or destructive.

Controllable Versus Uncontrollable

If you value something outside of your control it becomes very easy to give everything up for it. Money is probably the easiest or biggest example. While you may have some control over the income you make, you do not have total control over it. The economy can collapse.

Your company could go under. You could be laid off due to budget gets. Your job could be erased by technology. If everything that you do is all for the sake of money you can love what you perceive to be your purpose for living when tragedy strikes and consumes that money.

Money is a bad value because you cannot control money. What you can control, that still relates to money, is your work ethic, industriousness, ambition, or creativity. Those are good values because you control them. Money is a side effect of living out those values.

Healthy, controllable values include vulnerability, honesty, self-respect, humility, standing up for what you believe in, and curiosity.

Unhealthy, uncontrollable values include manipulation, violence, self-centeredness, the desire to be liked by everyone, and money.

Find Yourself

Have you ever noticed how there are things your body does automatically until you pay attention to them suddenly? You breathe without a second thought until you are focused on it. You automatically blink, swallow, and your heart does not need a reminder to beat. You do not generally pay much attention to your values until someone starts talking about values.

While some people may run away to find themselves, most of us remain trapped on the treadmill, forever running, never thinking about why you bother. There are questions to ask yourself that will help you find yourself and define your values.

Your personal values should serve as a measuring stick. The measuring stick you use to determine what a successful, meaningful life looks like.

What I Believe a Meaningful, Successful Life Looks Like

When you close your eyes, do you see yourself with a house filled in children and friends? Do you see yourself sashaying down a red-carpet answering media questions? Do you see yourself piloting a helicopter? Do you see yourself contributing to your community? How would you define a successful, meaningful life?

Do not judge yourself for the vision you create or how you answer the question. There will be time for that later. Just take it as it is and know it is important that you allow yourself the vision of what you genuinely desire. When your vision is clear you can move on to the next question.

> From That Life I Imagined, What Is It That Appeals to Me? What Is It That I Want?

Are you drawn to sashaying a red carpet because it would make you look cool or because it provides a good paycheck? Or are you simply interested in the attention that comes with it? When you ask yourself why you want the things you want it helps you identify the underlying values. You recognize you want to walk red carpets but dig deeper to determine what value is driving that want.

Now you can judge by asking whether the values you defined are bad or good. Now you can ask whether the values you defined are uncontrollable or controllable. Now you can question whether the values you defined are destructive or constructive. Now you can tease those values to determine whether they are emotion-based or evidence-based.

Would you happy to allow those values to guide you for the rest of your life? From here on out? If the answer is yes, then that is great. If the answer is no, you must hammer out some new values.

If you have been fully honest in answering the questions above, then you should have uncovered your values. But, if there's one thing we can know for certain is that we are adept at telling ourselves the stories that we want to hear rather than the stories we need to hear or stories that are true. You might say you want to walk red carpets. You might even be able to vividly picture yourself in designer wear, squinting at the flush bulbs of hundreds of cameras. But, if you spend the last decade or two of your life climbing the business ladder, your actions are in direct contradiction of your words. There is a disconnect.

The key thing to remember about values is your behavior is a constant reflection of them. Your values matter far more than the words you choose to say.

You can say you want a home filled with children; you can scream it from the rooftops that you value your family above everything else. However, if you find excuses to avoid serious relationships, then a family is not what you value.

So, ask those questions, and when you answer them be prepared to do a reality check. Do your stated values match with your actions? If there is a disconnect then ask yourself what you truly value.

Views of the World

Relationship to Self/Others Societal

Family   Caretaking Management
Beauty

Shelter/Food   Belief   Playfulness
Development

Obedience Fairness   Tradition   Intuition

Affection   Belonging Recognition
Collaboration

Curiosity   Loyalty   Self-Sacrifice
Equality

Safety   Discipline Stability
Community

Kindness Honesty Respect
Exploration

Self-Restraint   Duty Self-Worth
Empowerment

Wonder   Security   Righteousness
Integrity

Maintenance   Legacy   Self-Awareness
Independence

Sensuality   Patience   Justice
Sustainability

Equality   Dialogue   Service   Flexibility

Innovation   Expansion   Partnership
Strategy

Responsibility To Self/Others   Stability
Aspirational

Responsibility   Achievement   Charity
Detachment

Acceptance   Competence   Efficiency
Human rights

Being Present   Decisiveness   Authority
Altruism

Courage   Competition   Managing
Nonviolence

Diversity   Financial Success   Problem-Solving   Inspiring Others

Commitment   Hierarchical Ability   Patriotism   Reconciliation

Balance   Informing   Order   Spirituality

Choice   Productivity   Self-Confidence   Simplification

Empathy   Predictability   Rule of Law   Personal Growth

Creativity   Recreation   Quality   Meaning

Open-Mindedness   Rational Awareness   Rationality   Well-Being

Defining Your Values

Values are experience-based. So, just as you cannot argue someone else out of their values, neither can they argue yours out of yours. Trying to make people defensive and more resistant to change. When challenging values, one must do so with empathy, whether you are challenging yourself or someone else. The only way to let go of values that are failing you is to contradict them with evidence.

When you experience a value failure it can be scary, and you must allow yourself space to grieve. Your value contributes to the shaping of your identity and when a value is tumbled it can shake your understanding of who you are. It is almost like losing a piece of yourself. We feel compelled to resist a value failure by denying it or finding a way to explain it. We rationalize and we justify.

For example, you have spent two decades chasing money, and when you finally accumulated what you deemed to be enough you do not feel happy. In fact, you are more stressed out now because now you need to figure out how to spend it, where to invest it, and there are taxes to pay, and people who are always coming to you for handouts.

Rather than questioning the value that spurred you into accumulating the money you blame the government for punishing the wealthy, people for being lazy moochers, or the stock market. Ridiculous, right? The problem is not everyone else, it's a bad value.

Question your values and brainstorm which values would do a better job for you. Replace money as a value with freedom. Money does tie into that freedom, but it is not everything. Rather than setting a value of being liked, you could instead choose the value of intimacy by deepening your bonds with those closest to you. Instead of choosing the value of winning, you could choose the value of putting your best effort in always. Remember, values must be controllable.

It is all well and good to sit around thinking about better values. However, nothing will solidify it like choosing that value and going out to embody it. If you want to know whether a value truly works for you, then you must win or lose it through experience.

Forget your feelings, forget logic, and forget beliefs. Go and live those values. It might hurt at first, to live in opposition of old values, but you can. A little bit of fear is good, and it takes courage to act in the face of it. Is courage one of your values? Look at you, branching out already!

A Guide to Living Your Values

Choose a value, whether it is a brand-new value or an existing one you have decided to hold onto.

- Always choose goals that align with the value.

- Make your choices with your goals in mind. Every decision you make should edge you closer to achieving your goal.

- Draw on the physical and emotional benefits of your value and allow them to inspire you to continue pursuing that value.

- You did it, but now it is time to choose your next value and repeat the three steps above.

The steps are simple enough, but that does not mean they are easy. To do this you will have to step well outside your comfort zone, try things you have never done before, ditch a career you have invested half of your life in, or even upset some of the people you care about.

If you do not, then what is the point in uncovering your values to reinvent yourself? The alternative is remaining on autopilot and chasing a happiness you will never find because that happiness you are chasing is not real. It is not what you want, it is what you have convinced will suffice. Is that what life is about?

PART
6

Table of Contents

New Experiences	205
16 Ways To Learn And Broaden Your Horizons	210
Tourist Time	210
Explore A New Genre	211
Health And Happiness	213
Learn A Language	214
Explore Hobbies	215
Redecorate	216
Make Positive Change	218
Take It In-Depth	219
Random Reading	222
Random Viewing	224
A Page A Day	226
Deeper Conversation	227
Cultivate Your Curiosity	228
Strategize	230
New Routines	231
Miscellaneous	232

New Experiences

The older you get the more it seems as though your days merge into one long day. Over the years, you have developed a series of dislikes and likes, you think you have a good handle on what makes you happy, you can still experience childlike wonder when you experience something new that you feel passionate about.

But it gets more difficult to experience new things. Here is the thing, when you learn everything, you can and aim to constantly broaden your horizons, you will learn much more about yourself. Learning helps you move beyond fear, it helps you improve self-awareness, it helps you improve yourself. It is an investment in yourself.

You have likely heard influential people encourage you to do just that, to broaden your horizons. It does not matter whether it's a family member, or your favorite celebrity stopping by to sit on a late-night talk show couch.

It is something you have heard over and over and for a long time, you probably rolled your eyes... what does that even mean? The older we get the more it seems to fall into place as an important lesson you have long overlooked.

If you want a definition for the term to broaden your horizons, then it is simple. All it means is experiencing or learning about things you never have. It means opening your mind to other's opinions and new ideas. There are probably millions of ways for you to broaden your horizons, though some are easier and more common.

The most common, of course, is through travel. What better way to broaden your horizons than to step out of your comfort zone and zip code? As great as travel is for broadening your horizons, it is not affordable for everyone and that should not hold you back from expanding your horizons. You can travel your state if you have a small budget, but you have other options.

You can use travel as a metaphor and broaden your horizons by visiting the experiences and ideas that we pick up from traveling. For example, taking a French cooking class, trying cuisine from different countries whether it is using new recipes or ordering from the nearest restaurant. Perhaps you can travel to the wider area where you live. Or learn a new language. Read up about a country you have always wanted to visit, learn about their history, culture, and customs. Take a creative writing class that allows you to build your own worlds! You can travel without leaving the comfort of your own home.

No matter what way you choose to broaden your horizons, there is likely a need for courage. It takes courage to dive out of an airplane. Unless you have food issues, trying a new restaurant with a friend does not require all that much courage.

But it can be scary if it is something you have never experienced. When you join a new class, you could try sitting next to new people every week, you are constantly broadening your horizons within the context of broadening your horizons.

There are just some tasks that are easier than others, that is the way of life. However, if you do the smallest of these daily, you are constantly pushing yourself. You can make time for the big ones as often as possible.

Ultimately, no matter how big or small the task you choose is, you are required to leave your comfort zone in order to achieve it. And as we all know, sometimes leaving our comfort zone is the hardest thing to do.

It might seem intimidating, it might seem scary, especially when we spend so much time trying to conform to everyone else.

Start small. To gear up and get ready for it, I want you to remember how it felt the last time you enjoyed something new, and it went well and felt thrilling. Remember how nervous you felt beforehand, but how incredible you felt after.

Life moves so quickly, and the word will not stop turning and in a place of chaos where time seems to move quicker than before you must accelerate your personal growth. The only way to do that is to invest in yourself, learn everything you can, and broaden your horizons. Let us look at how!

16 Ways to Learn And Broaden Your Horizons

Tourist Time

If you do not have the time or money to explore the world, you can start your tourist journey much closer to home. Start with your own city but view it as a tourist would. Think of the art galleries, museums, and amusement parks closest to you.

The places you would go in your youth but have not bothered to revisit because you have done it before. It is time to revisit those hotspots and embrace your city through new eyes. When was the last time you went? Probably when someone visited from out of town.

As a teenager, we entertained a lot of guests from abroad and every visit resulted in getting dragged around every tourist hotspot across the area (and there were a lot of them). I stopped visiting those places as an adult. When I revisited one of them recently, I was bowled over by what I saw. I was retracing old steps, but looking at everything through new eyes, and in doing so I was broadening my horizons.

Plan your weekends to visit some of the most popular places around town. When you finish everything in your city, move onto the next city or another part of the state or a neighboring state. There is nothing wrong with traveling abroad or dreaming of doing so, but we often forget about all the experiences on our doorstep. This is your opportunity to explore your own culture and get to know the history and sights of your environment.

Explore A New Genre

What type of music do you generally listen to? There are so many different artists to explore, but if you have been locked in on country for decades it is time to explore outside of that. You will probably find there are a lot of genres you enjoy; you just haven't taken the chance to listen because you like what you like, and you've stuck to it. If you use an app like Spotify, it will sum up your listening habits for the year.

It will tell you how many new artists you have listened to, how many different artists you heard, and the number of genres you explored, too. It makes for fascinating data and it is a great way for you to see how far you pushed yourself out of your comfort zone. There is also the bonus of easily browsing a variety of genres and compilation playlists to get a taste of many related artists.

My daily playlist jumps from country to bubblegum pop to EDM to rap, hardcore punk, rock, indie, and even classical. I listened to almost 200 new artists in 2020, over 200 genres, and explored over 100 new genres.

The more you explore the more you find to enjoy. My top performing genres? Pop, country, rock, classical, and punk. I love music so I love exploring new artists, genres, and I think it is one of the greatest ways to broaden your horizons. Do not stop at English-speaking artists either, branch out even further. If you happen to be learning a new language, start with musicians who sing in it.

So, look out for live events in your area and explore new music as often as you can.

Health and Happiness

Your mind will thrive when you engage it. If you want to find health and happiness, then you need to seek out new, exciting activities. This is hugely beneficial to you, but especially as you mature and improve. If you live an incredibly busy, professional life, then you need a hobby completely unconnected to your professional side.

Some people cannot cope with being 'idle' and if that describes you, you need an activity that provides you with relaxation and action. Think of activities that stimulate your mind, like art appreciation.

If you want something to benefit your mind and your body, then consider a physical activity like a sport. If it is something entirely new to you and you are afraid of looking foolish, be sure to choose a physical activity where you are surrounded by people at the same level. You do not have to be perfect; it's about having fun and enjoying the activity just because.

Learn A Language

Have you ever wished you were bilingual? Or, even trilingual? Me too. There are plenty of free apps out there you can use to learn a new language and there are a lot of languages to choose from! If you want to ensure you take it seriously, enlist an accountability partner to join you on your journey.

Someone that will encourage you to do your daily lesson and someone you can speak to and chat within that language to practice and bolster your skills.

Listen to music in that language, watch television programs and movies in that language using the subtitles to enforce it. Learn more about the country, explore the culture, and push yourself to learn something new in the language every day.

Explore Hobbies

Could you make a list of your hobbies and easily identify when you last engaged in them? We have this nasty little habit of listing off hobbies and activities we enjoy and then realizing it has been years since we last practiced any of them.

Time tends to get away from us when life gets in the way. Think about a sport, artistic bent, or other activity you have always wanted to explore, but you never got the chance to as a child (or an adult). That might be exactly where to start, whether it is a beginner's jazz tap class, a bowling league, or even.

If it is something that takes a bit of talent, you can start with an online course to learn the basics before you branch out to join a proper class. If it is fun, then it is not a waste of your time. The entire point of hobbies and activities is that you enjoy them. The things you do with your spare time should bring you joy.

Redecorate

There has been a lot of conversation over the years about the link between psychology and interior design, specifically when it comes to colors. All over the world, police officers are often found in navy blue. The most intimidating soccer teams wear red. Hospitals are white, fast food outlets use reds, oranges, and yellows.

Have you ever done a bit of research into the colors you have used throughout your home? Have you tried to use colors to influence your mood and mindset? You don't have to be an interior designer to explore the meaning behind different color choices.

Broaden your horizons by exploring the psychology behind colors and using it in your own interior design to give your mood a boost! There is something powerful about redecorating, especially when it has been a while.

Make Positive Change

There are all types of positive changes you can make in your life, but in this case, what I am talking about is your diet. The food you eat fuels your body and mind. It influences your health. It can change your sleep pattern. It impacts the way you feel. So, I am not talking about going on a diet. What I am talking about is reassessing your dietary choices and making some tweaks to ensure you have a healthy lifestyle.

Pay attention to the foods you choose to eat daily. What impact do those foods have on your mind and body? What could you choose instead? Could you survive without eating those unhealthy options?

Look at the nutritional value of the food you buy and eat. Think about how much water you drink versus how much you should drink.

Make it your business to know what you are putting in your body because the more you learn everything you can about it the better placed you will be to make better decisions. You do not have to push your limits to eat better because this is not about following a restrictive diet, it is about making wiser decisions.

Since you are learning everything you can, you might as well take this opportunity to expand your horizons and try new fruits and vegetables when you see them appear in your local supermarket. There is always something random making an appearance, do not just stare at it making a face. Buy it and try it!

Take It In-Depth

How you choose to approach this learning project is entirely up to you. However, why not start with a topic of discussion that interests you, but you don't have an in-depth knowledge of it? Use the internet to research it. Make it your business to know everything you can possibly know. Just be sure to use reliable sources to gain that learning or you could end up achieving the opposite of your intention.

Alternatively, take a subject that you do know a lot about it and do some research into how you can express your opinion differently, whether it is using different vocabulary or coming at it from a different angle.

What is the point of this? Well, have you ever been to a social event and heard yourself talking about a topic you love and realized how dull it makes you sound? The other person might not find it dull, but you realize you have been wittering on uninterrupted for so long that you suddenly want the ground to open up and swallow you.

You question your level of engagement and compare yourself to other guests who share witty stories, cover interesting topics, and you feel out of your depth. Whether it's true or not, it can make you feel awkward.

By finding a different way to express your interest in a subject you do two things. Firstly, you indulge your passion for the topic and gain an even deeper knowledge of it. Secondly, you learn to think and see it differently and by addressing the way you discuss it and even how you think about it and interact with it.

You should not compare yourself to others, though, it's pointless. Especially, when this is something that you can control, and you can take it into your own hands.

Next up, think about a common topic of conversation that you are not particularly well-versed in. It should be a topic your nearest and dearest often broach and you sit back and clam up when it comes up.

Maybe it is something you're not interested in or you are interested, but you know everyone knows a lot about it and you're afraid to look foolish by chipping in. Read up on it and make yourself comfortable with every angle of the conversation and with the arguments that you have heard your friends/family make.

Now, your final goal on the subject is to learn five new words a day. Ideally, those words will be related to the subject that you're working on at the time. Make sure they stick by taking notes on what they mean, how they can be used in a sentence, the context of their use, and make it interesting by learning a bit about their etymology too.

Random Reading

Just like I encouraged you to get out of your comfort zone when it comes to your musical tastes, it is also wise to broaden your reading horizons! If you only ever read autobiographies, branch out by reading a romance novel! If you only ever read crime thrillers, try to embrace a psychology book or two.

There are so many different genres of books out there and you would be surprised what you might enjoy. The trouble is it is difficult to know where to start. I am going to help you with that.

You have two options. If you use social media, then sign up for a Goodreads account and link it. You will start getting regular updates from Goodreads about what your friends are reading and you can explore some new reading material that way.

Or you can take a more direct route and simply ask the readers in your friends and family for recommendations. You could also just ask them to lend you one of their favorite reads and do the same for them in return.

Whatever you do, do not make suggestions, do not tell them what themes you prefer, or the genres you normally read, just trust them with the choice.

Random Viewing

Continuing with the same theme, we tend to watch the same type of content and rarely break out of it even when certain programs take the world by storm. I, for one, have never seen a single episode of Game of Thrones and I have no interest in the fantasy genre whatsoever. I have had friends tell me repeatedly that I would love it and I have never once been tempted to watch it. I simply do not have the time to get tied up with such a backlog of content. I do, however, listen to other recommendations. I enjoy viewing things my friends enjoy and think, for whatever reason, that I would also get a kick out of. It is also a good way to get out of my viewing comfort zone and explore a bit.

Ask some of your friends and family what favorite movies, shows, and documentaries are streaming, and make a list of those you would never normally watch. You might not learn a lot about a particular subject, but you might learn something about your friends.

It might not be an educational piece of media, but it can enlighten you about different types of content. Or perhaps it will simply spark your creativity and get those juices flowing.

Finally, why not try some foreign content? Choose the shows or movies that remain in their original language and offer subtitles. This is especially useful if you are learning a new language. There is content from all over the world on most streaming services, so it is more attainable than ever before.

You just need to change the language settings. If you are learning Spanish, you can choose from Elite, Cable Girls, Money

Heist, The House of Flowers. Dark is available if you are learning German, The Rain if you are into Danish, and Norway's Home for the Holidays offers two seasons of holiday goodness.

A Page A Day

Whether you have encyclopedias around the house or need to take it online, choose a random page to read daily. Choose science, literature, philosophy, religion, geography, history, or anything you would like to learn more about. It doesn't take much time to read a page a day and you can read more if you like but aim for that first page and work on consistency.

If you have room in your book budget, there are plenty of 'devotional' style books that provide you a page of history (or other subjects) to read a day. They are not dated, simply marked with a day of the week so you can start them at any point. David S.

Kidder and Noah Oppenheim released a series of Intellectual Devotionals covering American History, Cultured Class, the World's Greatest Personalities and Wellness.

Deeper Conversation

You do not have to be sitting face to face to have a deep conversation with someone you love. You can use video chats, texts, emails, or even a phone call! So old-fashioned, right? Sometimes learning everything you can about a friend and what has been going on in their life, is a way of broadening your horizons. We build empathy when we actively listen to others share their lives, problems, and joy. Do not be afraid to continue building those relationships as a bid to expand your horizons.

You can also take things a step further by engaging with the children in your lives, whether they are your own or nieces and nephews. There is nothing more illuminating than having a conversation with the younger generations.

They are the most curious among us and because they are constantly learning, they have a lot to share whether we realize it or not. They also tend to ask an awful lot of questions, so you might just learn something about yourself under the interrogation of a mini adult.

Cultivate Your Curiosity

I just encouraged you to engage with children to enjoy their curiosity now it is your turn. It is time for you to cultivate your curiosity. In doing so, you learn everything you can and broaden your horizons.

Get curious about the way things work – what makes the water come on when you turn the tap, how do roller coasters move, what goes into the making of a smartphone, how does everything fit together to make a television work? Whatever it is, you should never be content with the things you already know, you should always look to learn more.

Another part of cultivating curiosity is constantly challenging your beliefs. What is one belief you hold that you know attracts debate? Go and read up on the debate. Do not just choose opinions of people you dislike, it is easier to dig in and dismiss those conversations.

Choose reliable sources, well-regarded voices, and even ask friends their opinions. It does not mean you should change your belief at the end of it, but you should at least interrogate the why behind your steadfast belief. If you do change your beliefs, that is great! It is not a weakness, it's a superpower.

Do you know what highly intelligent people do when they come across something they do not know? They seek the answer.

Do you know what people with less intelligence do when they come across something they do not know? They often pretend they do know it because they are convinced their lack of knowledge is a shameful thing.

A lack of knowledge is not shameful unless you refuse to grow. It is okay if you do not know things. It is not okay if you never bother to know things.

Strategize

Playing games might not seem like a learning opportunity or a way to broaden your horizons, but it certainly is if you choose the right games. For example, chess is great if you would like to improve your critical thinking.

Playing poker with company can help you improve your empathy because it is all about watching the nonverbal cues of other players. Charades can help you improve your communication skills because it forces you to use body language over your verbal skills. Even a game like Sims had its benefits, it is a great way to indulge your creative side whether it's in creating a Sim or building a masterpiece of a home.

New Routines

Routines are nice, they are comfortable. They help us manage our time more efficiently because with our brain running on autopilot for so many tasks, it frees us its power to be used as you deem necessary.

But it is important to change things up from time to time and create new routines too. Instead of rolling over to turn your alarm off and immediately open social media, why not get up and head for a shower immediately. Enjoy coffee and breakfast while you read something useful, listen to a podcast, or watch a documentary. Take a completely different route to work and explore your area instead of always sticking to the same parts of town. Eat lunch outside. Hey, have dessert before dinner! Mix things up a little and broaden your horizons.

Miscellaneous

Explore in the kitchen by trying out new foods and new recipes. It is not just getting a bit of culture and broadening your tastebud's horizons. It is also an opportunity for you to learn more about the food you put on your table.

Where did those tomatoes come from? How about your avocados? How far did these products travel to make it onto the local produce department you shopped? What type of processes do farmers use to harvest them? There is plenty you can learn.

If you happen to realize that much of your produce travels from far and wide, perhaps it is time to determine what you can start growing in your very own vegetable garden.

Some things, such as fruit trees, take years to produce fruit, but herbs like cilantro, vegetables like peppers, and fruits like tomatoes are all quick to produce the goods.

They also taste much better when you grow them at home. Even if you do not want to build an edible garden, gardening is fun. So, perhaps you would prefer flowers and plants. There is little more satisfying than seeing a seed you planted grow. It is great for relieving stress, it will boost your mood, and you are going to learn a lot about soil quality, how the weather influences certain plants, and so much more!

If you want to learn everything you can and broaden your horizons, then you must start by trying. And there is a good chance you will fail. The more you try, the more you will fail, but ultimately, that's part of the human process.

That's the beauty of life and though you may fail miserably and often, you live and you learn. With every failure you experience, you have a fresh opportunity to learn everything you can and certainly, with failure comes the chance to broaden your horizons.

Do not underestimate your ability to learn, just start investing in yourself.

PART 7

Table of Contents

How Do You Spend Your Time?	237
Your Time's Worth	238
The Dilemma	240
Calculate the Worth of Your Time	242
Using Your Time Wisely	248
Why Time Matters	252
Time Is Valuable	253
Life Is Unexpected	253
Time Is a Teacher	254
The Impact of Time	255
Time Heals	256
Time Is Binding	257
Time Is Inescapable	258
Time Is Powerful	258
Time Builds	259
Spending Your Time Well	259
Work Time	261
Invest in Yourself: Better Use of Your Time	263
54 Ideas of Time Better Spent	264
Avoiding Distractions and Disruptions	268

How Do You Spend Your Time?

You cannot buy more of it, there is only so many minutes in every day.

One of life's simple truths, even if it is hard to hear, is that not every use of time is equal. If you spend your time wisely then you will likely be a more profitable person, whether that is monetarily or otherwise. If you invest your time in others, then you are using your time to build stronger relationships.

If you use your time to build a high-flying career, then you will likely make more money. Likewise, if you invest your time in activities that contribute to your community, then you will leave a legacy. Whatever you want, whether it's freedom, wealth, friendship, or a legacy to be proud of, it all boils down to how wisely you spend your time.

Like most people, you probably want good health, great friendships, plenty of freedom, and societal impact. That is normal, but ultimately, you can't have it all. At least, not all at once. Therefore, you have to understand how to manage those tradeoffs that come up daily.

So, we are going to look at things differently. We're going to approach it from a monetary angle because what better way to understand just how valuable your time is than by expressing it in dollars and cents!

Your Time's Worth

Have you ever spent a considerable amount of time shopping for a specific item only to finally find it and it is a bargain? You just about jump for joy when you see the price and realize it is only $25! It is the affordable purchase you have been searching for, but wait, there is just one problem. It is a foreign seller, and the product is only $25, but the shipping cost alone is $50.

Imagine, spending $50 just for a $25 product to be shipped to you. It is downright egregious. So, you leave that bargain in the basket and you start searching the retail stores in your local area. You find one and you realize that the return journey would take two hours.

Was $50 worth two hours of your time? Spending $50 to have the product shipped to you would cost more than you planned to spend, but not all that much more than the product was retailing for. It is going to eat up so much of your time just traveling to get the product, time you could be spending better elsewhere.

Do you save the $50 and spend two hours traveling along with gas usage? Or do you spend the $50 to get the product delivered to your door with no more time-wasting?

Which one is a better use of your money and time?

The Dilemma

While you might not think about it often, there is a good chance you have a gauge for how much you believe your time to be worth. While this is an exaggeration, it is fair to say that if someone offered you $3,000 for an hour of work you would happily accept, but if they offered you a quarter for an hour of your time you would walk away offended.

It is easy to make a decision like that when the offers are on such intense ends of the spectrum. When you start nudging the needle toward the middle of that spectrum, however, the lines grow blurry. It is suddenly far less clear if a task is worth your time and energy or not. That is the problem. We live most of the life in the blurry lines of the spectrum.

For example, you could save two hours by paying up for the nonstop flight. But taking a layover means you save $100. Is $100 worth two hours of your time?

You could mow the lawn on Saturday morning, or you could pay the local landscaping teenager $25 to do it for you.

You could work with a client for a guaranteed $2,500 paycheck this week. Or you could choose your own business idea to work on and that may generate $30,000 in the next year.

Perhaps you spend $30 to order food in and save yourself time making dinner when you have had a rough day. Or you spend an hour cooking for everyone, save the $30, and probably eat something healthier.

These are the types of choices that you make every day. Most people make those decisions using guesswork, they do it on a gut instinct. Rarely does anyone stop to calculate how much their time is worth. The reality is, we all have an hourly rate. A value we will accept, but rarely can anyone tell you what their hourly rate is.

Calculate the Worth of Your Time

There are all different ways for you to calculate the worth of your time. The easiest way would you to work out your hourly rate based on the salary that you earn. It is even easier if you are paid hourly. Our employers do not always pay us our worth. So, let us work out what you are worth.

This first calculation should help you make smarter spending decisions like whether it is worth your time to spend $50 for shipping versus driving two hours to buy it in person.

All you need for this exercise is how much time you spend earning your money and how much you earn for working those hours.

We will use an imaginary number for this, but for you to calculate your working time is simple. How many hours do you work? You should include your commute because that is time invested in earning your wage. So, your commute is an hour a day and you work eight hours. That is a nine-hour workday. If you have a secondary income from a side hustle, then you should include all that information in your equations. You might have to spend some energy tracking your time because a lot of people have no idea how they spend their 24 hours each day.

So, for the sake of this exercise, we will say you spend 10 hours of your day involve with work and that adds up to 50 hours weekly, assuming you work five days. If you work 50 weeks of the year that adds up to 2,500 hours of work a year. It is fair to say that this number is in the ballpark for most full-time workers.

Now you need to look at how much money you earned for all that time you spend working. The easiest way to do so is to look at your most recent paycheck and then multiple it by whatever number of paychecks you receive each year. Alternatively, last year's tax return can help. The number you want is the take-home amount, after taxes, etc. has been deducted. It is what you effectively hold in your hand.

Now you just divide the money you earned by the time you spend working.

For example, you spent 2,500 hours working in the last year.

If your income was: $12,700, then your hourly rate is $5.08. This was the 2020 poverty line for a single person in the US, depending on the state you live in.

If your income was: $47,299, then your hourly rate is $18.92. This was the 2020 median income for women in the US. If your income was $57,456, then your hourly rate is $22.98. This was the 2020 median income for men in the US.

If your income was: $150,000, then your hourly rate is $60. If you make $1,000,000 annually, then your hourly rate is $400!

Of course, how this works out is entirely dependent on how many hours you work, how much you get paid, and whether you put in extra hours to generate additional income, and how much that additional income adds up to. You will need to do your own math.

Once you work out the value of an hour you might be surprised. You might think you're worth more. Maybe you are, but this is the reality of your situation.

Just think of the freelancers that set their hourly rate at $60 but earn nowhere near $150,000 annually. Or, the consultants or lawyers who charge $400, but fall spectacularly short of earning a million.

How is this possible?

They only earn that rate for some of the work they do, not all of it. That is the easiest way to explain it. You might have a firm grasp on what you would charge hourly but rarely do we calculate the effort that we put into earning money that falls outside of the typical working hours.

You get a much clearer view of things when you account for all the time you spend trying to earn money, as you were encouraged to do so above. Sadly, it generally comes out as much less than you would charge for an hour of work if you were on the clock.

Is the number you calculated correct, though? Because it does not feel right. It feels far too low.

You can double-check your work if you question it, but sadly, it is likely accurate. It might be even worse than you realize because there is a good chance you missed some of the extra work you put in and did not get paid for.

Now, let's look at how you can use that information.

Your math has suggested that your time is worth $25 hourly. Therefore, spending half an hour of your time lining up for a $10 gift card is not a good use of your time.

You have discovered your time is worth $60 an hour so $50 shipping is a way better use of your time than traveling two hours to purchase a $25 product.

You worked it out and your hourly rate is $80 so you will absolutely pay the extra cost for a nonstop flight. It is worth it.

Once you have a good idea of what your time is worth in dollars and cents it becomes much easier to ensure you spend that time wisely.

Using Your Time Wisely

When you decide how to spend your time it is important that you do not waste it focusing on the wrong things.

As important as it is to understand how valuable your time is, it is just as important that you understand what you want from life. Knowing the value of your time will not be particularly helpful if you do not know how to direct that knowledge.

A lot of people get caught up chasing approval, money, or power. Everyone else is doing it so it seems to make sense. But have you ever stopped to question whether that is what you want? Sure, you can focus on increasing the value of your time, but some people want more free time and are not concerned with the money aspect. That is what you need a good grip on your core values.

Bill Gates is so rich that his time is worth over $100 per second. Not every second that he is awake or working, every second of every day. If he dropped a $100, the very act of bending over to pick it up would technically be a waste of his time. Except, it is not really because while he is bending down to pick that money up, he is still earning more. He is not losing time and money by picking up the money he dropped. It is not a one or the other situation.

Though, many of the situations you face will be tradeoffs. Unless you are Bill Gates.

For example, an author who is also a motivational speaker. If they spend the majority of their time attending speaking engagements, then they will have far less time to write new books.

Eventually, they would be less relevant because they stopped producing new work to speak about. Therefore, their rate would decrease before eventually work would dry up entirely. So, an author must make plenty of time for writing to support the speaking engagements.

There is a danger to calculating your time value this way. It becomes much easier to talk yourself into using another hour productively to increase the value of your time. That can harm your quality of life. It is easy to get caught up in this behavior and the more often you do the less time you have to spend on rewarding activities.

You can track your free time to see how much of it you use for leisure versus work, but it is important that you do not put a value on that free time. You must think of it as non-negotiable time. Those free hours are valuable.

They are your opportunity to decompress, reenergize, and ensure that you have the energy and focus to use your productive hours wisely. Free time is valuable and it should be recreational. It should be the time you spend with family, engaging in activities you enjoy, catching up with friends, and just enjoying what you enjoy.

So, should you work another hour?

Take a look at every hour of your day and how you spend it. Then look at each hour individually and ask yourself whether that block of time required net negative or net positive decisions. If you work an hour longer will you create positive outcomes with it? Or are you going to make more mistakes that you need to fix tomorrow?

Are you tired enough that an extra hour of work will get you nowhere fast? An extra hour of work isn't a positive choice if it results in burn out or a net negative on average.

Time is valuable no matter who you calculate its worth, when you consider how to invest in yourself for a better future, then how you spend your time is a key consideration because what you do today can predict and mold your tomorrows.

Why Time Matters

Now that we have addressed the value of your time, let us talk about why time matters aside from that. It is important because we often miss out on the benefits that come with time.

For example, can you think of the last time you carved out time for self-care?

If you regularly set half an hour aside to focus solely on your needs, you clearly recognize the value of your time and the importance of using some of that time to ensure you are in tip-top shape. It is a meaningful way to create a balanced life.

Time Is Valuable

You might not be able to physically hold it in your hands, but time is valuable. And, in many ways, its importance far exceeds the monetary value you worked out earlier. There is one thing that time and money have in common, you can save it. Or you can waste it. There is one major thing, though, they do not have in common. Once it is gone, you cannot get time back, but you can always earn more money.

Life Is Unexpected

You do not know the number of days you have to live on this earth nor do you know the number of days your loved ones have on this earth.

The person closest to you could be gone tomorrow and the last words you spoke to each other could have been in the heat of an argument. Those would be the last things you ever speak to each other and then they are gone.

That is not to say you should be a doormat for others, but it should highlight just how important it is to manage your emotions and be careful with your words. And, how important it is to spend time with the people you care about.

Likewise, you could wake up with a headache tomorrow and find out you have a terminal illness. We do not have time to waste in this life, we only get one chance to get it right. Having said that, do not attempt to live each day as though it is your last because that will only result in impulsive, potentially dangerous decisions. But, if you have a habit of overthinking everything, you will need to find a way to streamline your decision-making process.

Time Is a Teacher

Time is one of the greatest teachers because, with time, we recognize that though we may make mistakes, there is always a lesson to learn. Experience is what helps build morals, it is what shapes and builds character.

The Impact of Time

How you spend your time will affect you and the people you choose to spend your time with can change you. If you spend all your spare time watching movies, then you will be incredibly skilled at watching movies, analyzing them, breaking them down, and recommending them to your friends.

But, if you used that same amount of time for a productive task, then you will grow proficient at something useful. If you want to get good at something, learn more, understand more, then you must put time and effort into making it so. That is not to say you have to stop watching movies entirely, of course, it's simply that you should carve out free time to watch movies, and time for more productive uses.

The same is true of the people you spend your time with. Your friends rub off on you.

Their values influence you, whether it is in a positively or negatively. They may help you avoid riskier decisions. Or they might help you justify bad behavior.

Time Heals

Think of a painful experience from your past. Ideally, something that happens over five years ago. Even better if it was more than ten years ago. The pain you feel thinking about those moments now is nothing like the pain you felt when you went through it or even in the year following it. It might not go away entirely, but time does heal and it dulls the pain.

Time Is Binding

While OK Boomer became a meme, there is something important to touch on. Time binds us to people who were born in the same era. The simple reason for this is, though our experiences may vary wildly, there are lots of collective experiences we share with the people born during the same time.

You do not have to know someone to relate to someone born at a similar time. The struggles that Boomers faced are nowhere near the same type of struggles that Millennials have faced. Likewise, the struggles that Generation Z will deal with are nothing like those of Millennials. There is also a vast difference in morals from generation to generation, that is something that has and will always exist. Time binds you to others.

Time Is Inescapable

Time is limited, you cannot escape it. Everything ages, from humans to animals, to nature, to manmade objects. There is absolutely nothing in this world or in this life that is permanent.

Time Is Powerful

Time is powerful and how you choose to spend it can be powerful. When you spend some of your time serving others, then that is time well spent and it is time you are using powerfully. It also showers how important and powerful time is when you consider how little of it it takes to help someone.

You took 15 minutes to hear what is bothering your colleague and changed the course of their week, allowing them to get their head on straight. You spent an hour putting together care packages and an hour delivering them to the homeless community.

You have provided them with a bit of relief, saw to some of their needs, and let them know people care. You spent twenty minutes helping your child with their homework, a nice reminder that they are loved and that you want to help them learn and understand.

Time Builds

With time, comes stronger bonds and relationships. Time provides you with an opportunity to get to know someone, to build trust, to develop intimacy, and to grow closer to them. The longer you have, the stronger that relationship grows. The world would be a lonely place without friends.

Spending Your Time Well

You are faced with a multitude of decisions daily, but the ones you make involving your time are some of the most important. The only person who can determine what is classed as spending your time wisely is you.

We all have our own priorities and expectations, but it is fair to say that there are three key values everyone tends to agree on.

- People

People matter, whether it is practicing self-care to keep yourself on the level of feeling the gratifying reward of helping others. Time spent on yourself or others is always time well spent.

- Knowledge

The present is always greater than the past, just like the future should be. Humanity has made constant progress, with technological, scientific, and medical progress. Using your time to progress your own knowledge is always time well spent.

- Freedom

There are a variety of ways to look at freedom. Ultimately, being able to do the things you want to do, live the life you would like to live, and empower others to do the same... that is what freedom boils down to. You just must figure out how best to spend your time to further your specific idea of freedom.

Work Time

We talk a lot about striking a healthy work-life balance, but it is important to highlight the fact that a balance does not necessarily mean a 50-50 split. It is up to you to decide which split is the best use of your time. Only you can answer that question because it must align with your values.

Your life is important and spending your time well means protecting both your physical and mental health. In doing so, you protect your ability to invest time in work to earn money to pay your bills. You cannot ignore either side of things. Think of work as a way to contribute to your life and make those important decisions about your time from there.

So, how much time should you spend working?

As much as it takes to meet your needs. This, of course, will vary wildly depending on your job, but if you consistently work far more than you want to you should look at how to change that. Maybe you need to invest more of your free time into adding to your skill set or knowledge in order to change careers.

If you hate your job, work 60 hours a week, and you're still scraping by... then I can understand how easy it is to get up spending all your spare time playing video games to decompress or with your family because you have little time to spare. But it will always be this way if you do not use some of your spare time to further yourself. The choice is yours.

What do I do with the rest of my time?

What do you want to do?

The freedom to decide is all yours. However, there is an obligation with that freedom. You are obligated to use your time wisely. The only way to achieve that is to get a clear view of your values in order to prioritize your time accordingly.

Invest in Yourself: Better Use Of Your Time

Let's explore the concept that time is valuable. Life is short, we only have so much time in a day, and so much time in life. Considering how you spend that time from the aspect of investing in yourself is an important consideration.

Stop for a moment and think about you greatest time wasters, what are they? What could you do instead that promotes your wellbeing and a better future? Here are a few ideas:

54 Ideas of Time Better Spent

1. Research and list books, you want to read - make at least 3 of them educational

2. Read

3. Learn a new skill

4. Learn a language

5. Learn to plan an instrument

6. Do your own oil change in your car

7. Garden

8. Think about what matters most to you

9. Think about what you want your future life to be

10. Think about what you want your future self to be

11. Find an opportunity to speak in public

12. Watch a documentary

13. Create a vision board

14.   Listen to uplifting, motivational podcasts

15.   Make a plan with steps on how you will promote positive thinking within yourself

16.   Create a productive morning ritual

17.   Play brain games

18.   Make your "I Will Be More Productive" Plan

19.   Write a list of what fulfills you

20.   Write your "Life Mission Statement"

21.   Make a list of poor habits you need to change. Plan to change them.

22.   List all your resentments and plan to work through them

23.   Lie on the roof and watch the stars

24.   Set up a tent in the backyard and camp out

25. Spend quality time with your significant other

26. Spend quality time with your kids

27. Spend quality time with your pets

28. Turn off your brain

29. Update your resume and portfolio

30. Complete personal development workbooks

31. Watch motivational YouTube videos

32. Unfollow all negative, non-constructive people and channels from your social media account

33. Write out your "No List" - list of all the things you never want to do

34. Write out your "worry list" and burn it

35. Engage in a creative activity

36. Plan 10 actions you can take today that will improve your tomorrows

37. Write a letter to yourself in 5 years, 10 years, and 20 years

38. Do some financial planning

39. Exercise

40. Set goals and plans to achieve them

41. Rest, relax, turn off all electronics, slow down

42. Self-improvement activities

43. Meditation and Yoga

44. Take a class

45. Volunteer

46. Spend time with friends or family

47. Cultivate social connections

48. Consider your health

49. Learn to cook healthy

50. Network

51. Organize your spaces

52. Go to a museum

53. Blog

54. Journal

Avoiding Distractions and Disruptions

If you want to avoid disruptions and distractions, then you should take steps to eliminate those disruptions and distractions. For example, if emails, phone calls, and texts constantly interrupt you, whether at work or at play, then turn off notifications.

You don't need constant popups on your laptop or computer. Set a time for checking emails and restrict any email communication to that specific block of time. If much of your business is email related, set two blocks of email times.

You can use an app to block your use of specific apps during specific hours, which should help you avoid games, social media, and texts during hours you need focus.

It would behoove you to schedule your time. This process allows you to block time off for everything. Begin with a blank calendar or a spreadsheet that breaks your week down into hourly slots.

Create your schedule in the following order to ensure you consider your true priorities.

- Family/friend time is always first because that is crucial to both your mental and physical health. Your family and friends are the people closest to you and when they are gone, you will never get them back. Use your time wisely.

- Exercise time because it is important to look after your physical health which also protects your mental health. Exercising regularly helps prevent lifestyle diseases, improves mood, and helps stave off stress, anxiety, and depression.

- Recreational time for creating, reading, and thinking. This is the free time that you are using wisely and productively.

So, it is not technically free time, but it is time you can enjoy provided you are funneling your energy and focus appropriately.

- Free time, the time you spend relaxing and having fun, whether it is watching television, playing video games, taking a hot bath, or just sitting quietly and enjoying some peace and quiet.

- Work. Your work is important because it pays your bills, but if you start your schedule with work you will overdo it and end up with no time for anything else. Your job should have set hours and therefore, your work meetings and to-dos should fit into those working hours.

PART 8

Table of Contents

What Is Missing	273
The Help of Quality People	277
Letting Go	279
Surrounded by Elevation	281
Surrounded by Success	283
Surrounded by Discomfort	284
Surrounded by Greatness	285
Cultivating Real Relationships	288
Observe When You Can't Engag	289
Attracting the Right People	291
Self-Belief	293
Freely Forgive	294
Like For Like	294
Addressing Naysayers	295
Protect Your Goals	296
Consider the Source	297
Analyze the Message	299
Tune It Out, Refuse to Engage	299
Enablers	301
Your Vision	301
Show the Red Card	302

What Is Missing

Everyone wants to taste success, whether it be in romantic relationships, finances, emotional health, or friendship. There are all different aspects of life to consider, and we want to feel fulfilled in most of them. The problem is that most people find themselves lacking in one or more aspects of life.

Why? The biggest reason for a lack of fulfillment in life is low standards.

If there is one thing that can impact every aspect of your life and change it, your business prospects, your financial state, and the health of your relationships... it is your standards.

I would like you to think about the people you spend most of your time with. Who do you work with? Who do you date? What is your partner like? What type of people do you call a friend? It might just be that they all have something in common. They are negative. They are pessimists. They are naysaying, toxic people who are dragging you down.

It is hard to face up to the idea that your standards in people have been holding you back. Just as holding too high a standard for yourself leads to you holding others up to impossible standards, the opposite is true. When your standards are not high enough you attract people with impossibly low standards. Whether it is a conscious choice or not, they will do anything to keep you down at the same level as them. This isn't about holding your inner circle to impossible standards, it's about raising your standards and finding an inner circle that matches that energy.

Some people would say this is the law of attraction in its simplest form. There is an excellent quote that sums it up, and while Goodreads attributes it to Confucius, there is no way to determine where it originated. Regardless, the point stands:

"If you are the smartest person in the room, then you are in the wrong room."

Life is about growth and every single day you wake up is a fresh opportunity to stretch yourself and improve. When you are the smartest person in the room it is probably because you orchestrated it as such. You have chosen the room because you know you are head and shoulders above everyone else. After all, it makes you feel good. It is the same as the person who seeks out romantic partners who have less education and life experience. It was not a coincidence. If you look back at their dating history you will see a pattern. They have a need to feel superior and the way they do so is by surrounding themselves with people they deem less intelligent. That way, they always feel intelligent which makes them feel more confident.

It is an illusion.

They are not highly intelligent, they are simply more intelligent than the people they hang out with which is an intentional move to feel more intelligent. They are not truly more confident as soon as they find themselves in an unfamiliar situation that confidence pops like a balloon.

If you have ever done this or felt this way, then you know that you have intentionally allowed your standards to dip in order to attract the wrong people so you feel better about yourself.

That is the thing. Some people are unaware of their low standards, and some do it consciously. Though both are a form of self-sabotage, the latter is unconscious self-sabotage.

The Help of Quality People

One of the greatest ways that you can invest in yourself is by surrounding yourself with the right people - Winners, Supporters And Optimists.

The people you spend a lot of time with can have a major influence on your mood. They impact how you see the world. They can even prejudice how you see yourself and the expectations you hold for both yourself and others.

If you choose to surround yourself with only positive people, then you are more likely to embrace empowering beliefs. You are more likely to see life as something that is happening for you rather than to you. Positive people make you feel happier, negative people do not. Positive people make you more open-minded, negative people do not.

Think of a highly positive friend and how you feel after spending time with them versus an incredibly negative friend and how you feel after spending time with them... you know there is a difference, don't you? You know there are friends or family members you walk away from feeling empowered and uplifted.

Just as you know there are friends or family members you feel drained by when you walk away. You groan when their name pops up on your phone screen, whether it is a phone call or a simple text message.

The people you spend most of your time with, that is the type of person you will eventually become.

If you want to reach success, new heights, or otherwise, then you need to surround yourself with inspiring people. People who are positive but challenge you.

Letting Go

Do you think of yourself as a go-getter? Is your partner, team, or business partner someone who lacks ambition? Are you trying to feel your way to the next level of success, but you feel tugging from where those people have a hand on the back of your shirt holding you back. The first step to making changes to your friend group is to identify the people who bring you down or hold you back.

It might hurt, but it is important that you let go of those negative relationships. The more negative relationships you can let go of the easier it is to embrace new positive people and build those relationships.

How do you determine who is negative or toxic? You must think about how you feel after you spend time with them, speak to them, or text them. Do you feel good? About yourself, life, or in general? Do you feel ready to tackle any challenge? Or do you feel caught up in your emotions, upset, unsure, and uncomfortable?

Your emotions exist to communicate with you. Think of them as a gift to inform you of what is going on inside you. Your feelings will not always be factual, but they are valid and the more in touch you are with them, the easier it will be to read them accurately. So, if you feel agitated, drained, or fearful after you spend time with someone, then recognize that this person is not good for you.

It is uncomfortable to step away from the relationships you identify as lacking, toxic, or negative, for a host of reasons. Perhaps it is a childhood friend, maybe it is a family member, it could be a colleague you will still have to see at work every day. You cannot always burn bridges because sometimes there are obligations you cannot bow out of. You can put distance between the two of you while maintaining professional courtesy.

It is always particularly challenging when dealing with family and co-workers. The former because there are always other family members willing to go to bat for that person and guilt you into making a different decision. The latter because you still must work with them, even if you want to cut them off from your personal life.

If you are having trouble with cutting certain people off, then you need to dig deep and question why you feel the need to stay in those relationships. The only way to escape them is to get to the root of it, change your mindset, and let go.

Surrounded by Elevation

Everyone has goals. Whether it is to make it to the weekend, to finish the project you are working on right now, or to have a million dollars in your bank account before you are 50. There are goals and dreams of all sizes and shapes because there are people of all sizes and shapes. You do not have just one goal, though, do you? So, think about all the goals you have floating around in your mind or recorded on an action plan. Which of these goals is an absolute must? Where you invest your time and energy, those are the pursuits that directly reflect your standards. Just like your relationships do.

If your goal is to grow your business prospects, then why on earth would you be spending time with people who are negative? Why would you hang around those who distract you and put down your ideas?

Perhaps you are just used to certain people being in your life and you are concerned about moving on. Maybe you've just never thought about it before and you didn't realize how much of a negative impact certain people were having on you. Regardless, you should not allow fear or a lack of awareness to derail your success story.

You have the power to actively choose the people you spend time with and you can choose people who share your ambitions, empower you, make you feel happy, and push you to improve your standards.

Surrounded by Success

If you want to succeed, then you have to endeavor to never be the smartest person in the room. You want to surround yourself with people who stretch you and force you to grow. People who you can learn from.

Whether you join a community of people, many of whom have already achieved your goal, or you start attending relevant conferences as a way to network with successful people. If you cannot find them in your existing circles, then you simply need to expand those circles and cast a wider next.

When you do, look at how those people respond when faced with conflict. Consider how they network and build relationships with potential associates, as well as key contacts. What established habits have contributed to their success? Pay attention and learn.

Surrounded by Discomfort

How big (or small) is your comfort zone? If you surround yourself with people who live well within their comfort zone, then you will always live well within your comfort zone. It is the natural order of things.

Ambitious people go to workshops, attend seminars, and constantly seek knowledge because they want to stretch themselves as much as possible. They are prepared to expose themselves to differing views, contrary opinions, and alternative perspectives. They push themselves beyond their comfort zone and they do it consistently and continually.

If you surround yourself with the best in your industry, the best at what you want to do, then you are going to constantly push yourself to be better than you currently are.

Surrounded by Greatness

If you want to be the smartest person in every room and on every topic, you are strictly limiting yourself. It was the late Jim Rohn, a businessman and author, who said "You're the average of the five people you spend most of your time with."

There is no better way to sum it up than that. You are the average of five people, so who do you spend most of your time with? Is it people who challenge you? People who push you? People who constantly set the bar higher?

If you want to be a master chess player, then you need to play chess with people who do it better than you. Professional tennis players play against each other in competition and in practice.

Boxers do not just see each other when the bell rings, or in the press conferences running up to it. They enlist great boxers to spar with to prepare for the big bout. It does not matter whether you want to play better poker, improve your trivia skills, or become a master yogi. Whatever you want to do, you must grow by relying on people that are better than you. It is as simple as that. Whether you are at work or at play, surround yourself with winners. Surround yourself with people who are better than you.

You will always come across people constantly plagued by drama. You know the type, the people who are in constant turmoil and trap themselves in pity, never moving beyond their current position.

Life is tough, it is hard enough without having others trying to drag you down to their level. Once you cut those people out of your life, you will have to constantly set and maintain your boundaries to ensure that more of those people do not find their way into your circle. It will be a constant battle because as you socialize and network you will meet more people who will introduce you to more people.

You may have a positive interaction with someone upon first meeting, perhaps even multiple meetings. However, when the red flags of toxicity rear their ugly heads you must be prepared to take action.

You cannot always win. And, on your path to success, you will run into naysayers, negativity, and obstacles. When you do, there is nothing more satisfying than someone who is ready to listen to your fears and doubts. That is not enough. They cannot just listen. It is just as important that they cheer you on and motivate you to do better.

Our friends and family should be cheerleaders (and you should be the same for them). But even cheerleaders must get tough with the chips are down. Those are the relationships you should focus on. The people who propel and energize you.

Cultivating Real Relationships

Social media has its uses, but it has grown far too intertwined in our lives. For many, they have taken over the real relationships we have. Social media can also be a difficult reminder of the things you wanted to do but did not. The things you would like to have, but do not. Or the things that you wanted to accomplish, but not only have you not but someone else has. It can be difficult, especially when you watch someone else's stories or to see all these incredible adventures they are having.

You see the adventures, that is just the highlights. You do not see the work that went in behind the scenes. You do not see the breakdowns, fights, tears, and sweat that went into achieving it. You get to see the pretty picture they want to share, not the effort and strife that came with it. Social media focuses on the result, but you need to focus on the process.

Observe When You Can't Engage

Not everything is nearby or in front of your face to engage with. Sometimes, you must make do with what you can and that means observing. For example, a person desperate to play a sport can watch that sport when they are unable to actively engage in it.

There is a reason that football coaches show their team highlights of the competition. It is not just about practicing the plays they plan to employ to stop the other team. It is about seeing them in action and understanding how they play.

Likewise, not everyone can go to conferences and network with movers and shakers. There are monetary obstacles, as well as scheduling problems. That does not mean you should miss out on everything just because you do not have direct access.

That is your opportunity to watch webinars, to subscribe to relevant blogs, to listen to podcasts that offer knowledge.

The same is true for the people you surround yourself with. You might not know or have access to high-performing people. If you cannot get to them in person, you can go to where they spend their time online.

That is where social media is useful. Consume the thoughts and advice of highly successful people. You can listen to a podcast on your commute. You reach watch webinars in your spare time, read books, and observe.

Attracting the Right People

I have spoken at length about the time-bandits, energy suckers, and emotional vampires you need to cut from your life. I have touched on the type of people you want to attract and where you might find them.

Those time-bandits, energy suckers, and emotional vampires are a reflection of the incorrect stories you have told yourself that turned into limiting beliefs. They are a mirror of your insecurities. But it is up to you to change who you attract and how they interact with you. To do so you must first change how you feel and think about yourself.

Before you can start changing and improving your relationships you must work on your self-image. Everyone has a vibe. Other people pick up on that vibe. Have you ever met someone and had an immediate spark, platonic or otherwise?

A spark that made you realize that this was your kind of person? The start of a beautiful friendship. If your self-imagine is low then you will emit negative vibes, but when your self-image is flying high your vibes will be feel-good! Those vibes attract people. Just as feel-good vibes attract people with feel-good vibes so do bad vibes attract people with bad vibes.

The more people with bad vibes you attract the more you will draw negative experiences to you. This will simply validate your feelings that you are a victim, that the world is awful, and that nothing good can happen.

If you want to attract positive people, then you must start with yourself. You need to be a more positive person. You must think more positively about your life and your future. You can start by being grateful which means you need to review your life and find all the different things you feel grateful for.

Those are the things you can focus on while you work on becoming a more positive person. Now, let us look at a few ways you can easily attract naturally positive people.

Self-Belief

People can feel it, whether you believe in yourself or not. If you do not, then you will likely attract other people who also struggle with self-belief. Start believing in everything you are, it begins with total acceptance.

Your talents, strengths, attributes, gifts, and even your physical traits. Accept all of it. Show yourself kindness. Correct negative thoughts, correct negative self-talk, embrace positive self-talk, use positive affirmations, and honor yourself, your wants, desires, and truths. That will attract positive people.

Freely Forgive

A lack of forgiveness, whether it's toward others or yourself, is negative energy that will hold you back and attract more negativity. If you have made a mistake, accept that you have and forgive yourself for it. If someone else has harmed you, betrayed you, or cause you any type of emotional pain, then let go of the anger you have been holding onto.

Forgiveness is not about letting others off the hook. Forgiveness is beneficial to you and allows you to move forward. You do not have to let that person back in. You do not have to have a conversation with them. You only need to make peace within yourself and move forward.

Like for Like

If you want to attract positive people and positive experiences, you need to feel positive about yourself and your life. You must look at your past as an opportunity for learning. You must view your current situation as a chance to grow and your chance to shape your future. That positive mindset is what will help attract positive situations and people to you.

If there are positive relationships in your life, embrace them. If there are inspirational people in your life, embrace them. The people who motivate and empower you, embrace them! You should also do the same in return. Celebrate when others succeed. Celebrate your own successes.

Pay attention to your thoughts, if they veer to the negative gently correct them with positive thoughts. Self-believe and self-love should become a daily practice.

Addressing Naysayers

The naysayer who constantly puts your ideas down. The negative nelly who laughs in response to your suggestions and tells you your dreams are impossible. The pessimist who is not above sabotaging you when good things start to happen. What do you do with them?

Protect Your Goals

If you try to erect a house of cards during strong wind, how far do you think you will get? You are not going to get far, but you will get frustrated. Think of naysayers as the wind and your big ideas as the house of cards you have been trying to build. Your efforts will be in vain if you do not take steps to protect them.

The naysays focus on all the dangers and the downsides, they are skeptical and discouraging. They are quick to offer anecdotal stories of failure somewhere related to your goal. Every second you sit and listen is like another strong gust of wind coming for your house of cards. In the end, you have lost all self-confidence and you wonder whether you should go through with it.

But before you spoke to this person you felt optimistic! You were flying high, confident that you could do this. Your goals matter too much to allow others the power to taint them. Protect your goals and do not let naysayers have the chance to damage them. If you know a naysayer, do not share your ideas or goals with them.

Consider the Source

Before you even consider heeding someone's advice, you must consider the source. Is the person offering advice living the type of life you want for yourself? Is the person offering advice successful in what you are pursuing?

Or do they have any relevant experience? Does the person offering you advice have expertise or knowledge in what they are speaking about? The answers to those questions can help you determine whether the source is a worthy one.

If you want to eat well and lose weight, but an overweight colleague who follows every fad diet going wants to offer advice… it is probably best to ignore them. Unless they are warning you off a specific fad diet.

Then they may be speaking the truth. If you are starting a business and your friend is offering advice even though they have never started a business or worked in the industry of your focus… you can pretty much ignore everything they have to say.

If you are desperate to quit smoking, but your smoking friends try to warn you about how hard it is… they are not wrong, it is hard, but they're not great sources of advice on the subject.

Analyze the Message

When you are dealing with a naysayer, pay attention to their message and the words they use.

- Does what they are saying resonate with you?
- Is there any validity to their words?
- Will you be better off if you apply this advice?
- Is this person coming from a place of love? Or are they coming from a place of fear?

If you answer no to any of these questions, then this is likely advice you can ignore. Even though they may believe it is well-intended.

Tune It Out, Refuse to Engage

If someone is offering bad advice or is just discouraging in general, then you must tune it and them out. Just because someone is willing to offer you advice does not mean that you are beholden to take it.

If you have an idea, you have done the research, consulted with experts, and gone to great length to put a plan together, you do not need to listen to a naysayer standing by to tell you that you are wrong. Provided your ideas, goals, or plans are informed, then the only advice you need is from experts. The only approval you need to seek is the people who would be directly impacted by the decision or plan you have put together.

Additionally, it is important that you know that naysayers are as resolute in their views as you are staunch about your goals. Do not engage in their discussions. You do not have to fight back or justify your stance. It is a waste of time and energy.

Enablers

When we talk about enabling and enablers it is generally a negative thing. But, in this context, you need people who enable you to do positive things. People who encourage you, build you up and motivate you. Those are the people you should surround yourself with. There is nothing worse than having no one to turn to when you need help. Think of who can help and build those relationships.

Your Vision

If you were to imagine your ideal life, what does that vision look like? When naysayers distract you it is probably because you took your eye off that vision. Push your focus back to your vision and think about what it is you want to achieve. What do you want out of life? Is the opinion of a naysayer worth derailing that? No. Don't let a naysayer put you off your purpose.

Show the Red Card

If you can, show naysayers in your life the red card. You do not have to engage with people who only want to put your ideas down. The best course of action in dealing with people trying to darken your worldview is to remove them from your life entirely. If that is not possible, reduce contact as much as possible.

If it is a colleague, spend your time with other co-workers. If it is a friend, spend your time with different friends. If it is a family member, you don't have to spend time with them if you don't want to. When you are forced to, you can engage in subjects unrelated to your goals.

Surrounding yourself with the right people is a key investment in your future, get started today!

PART 9

Table of Contents

Personal Development Investment in Your Future	305
Your Personal Development Plan	307
What to Include	307
Tracking Your Progress	309
What to Consider	310
The Benefits of a Personal Development Plan	312
The Truth About Personal Development	314
Why should you sit down and create a personal development plan?	314
Why You Don't Need A Personal Development Plan	317
The Elements Of A Personal Development Plan	318
Clarity	318
Understanding	319
Standards	321
Priorities	322
Details	323
The Benefits of Personal Development	324
Final Thoughts	334

Personal Development Is an Investment in Your Future

When you are chasing your dreams and pursuing your passion it can be difficult to maintain your motivation. You have always thought of yourself as an ambitious person, but you have noticed just how difficult it is to keep your motivation and energy levels at the same level as it was when you started the journey. If you want to invest in yourself and turn your future goals into a reality, then you need a personal development plan.

A personal development plan will provide you with structure. It will help you remain proactive. It will push you to take consistent steps forward to achieve your goals.

A personal development plan is an investment in your future.

It is always time for a personal development plan. You can create one whenever you like, at any time in your life. It's all about making goals that are specific to you and your situation.

There is a good chance you have created something of the sort at work and your manager likely led the process. They hold your reviews and identify your weaknesses, trying to pull a plan together for you to improve on those weaknesses. It is all about identifying key areas to focus on and having a clear plan on how you can do that.

You do not need your boss on hand to create your own PDP, whether it is related to work or not. If your PDP is work-related and you have a great boss, then you may want to enlist their help or ask for their advice. There is nothing wrong with that.

Before you can even think about what a personal development plan looks like, let us talk about what it is.

Your Personal Development Plan

Also referred to as a PDP, the personal development plan is essentially a written record or account of improvement and self-reflection. It doubles as an action plan that is used to fulfill goals, whether they be career-based, academic, or personal. It is generally created in a working environment, your employer may be involved in the process. The purpose of creating a PDP is to establish aims, highlight weaknesses, recognize strengths, as well as identify areas for improvement.

Objectives are then put in place depending on where you want to improve. It is made up of your personalized actions that will ensure you meet those objectives.

What to Include

You must accurately outline all your personal goals, that doesn't just include what they are, it should also include how you plan to achieve them and why you want to achieve them. Every PDP looks different because they are unique to the person who creates them.

However, they all generally serve the same purpose, which is to detail your ideal future using short-term goals and long-term ambitions to shape how you spend your time and focus your energy. The areas of development you focus on will depend on your wants, needs, and desires. For you, it could be a focus on self-improvement, with a touch of focus on work or education.

A personal development plan also needs to recognize any potential obstacles or challenges that you may run into. You cannot just make a note of them, though, you have to take the next step which is to determine how you can best overcome them.

Or, if an obstacle cannot be overcome you need a contingency plan to manage it as effectively as possible, so it does not derail your efforts entirely.

Tracking Your Progress

There is no point putting all that work into creating a personal development plan if you do not also have a plan in place to track your progress. Like any action or development plan, there should always be a timeframe or time limit.

Having time attached to every goal helps you maintain your motivation to achieve it on time. It also ensures you do not ignore certain things that aren't as enjoyable as others.

A PDP is an efficient way to track your progress and measure your success. You can use it to demonstrate your skills and knowledge and as a motivational tool to keep pushing. You can review it and update it as regularly as you need.

Just ensure you set realistic goals with clear (and achievable) timelines. If there is a goal you keep writing down even though you know it is so farfetched it is impossible for you to make it happen no matter how hard you plan, you will need to find a compromise or let it go. A good example of a farfetched plan would be I will be a billionaire before I retire. It is unlikely.

What to Consider

You can use a PDP for just about anything. If you want to progress your career, then a personal development plan is a useful tool. You are interested in making a career change? Then a PDP is a must.

You might be thinking about moving back into education and you will need a personal development plan to help you manage the change. Perhaps, you're interested in a PDP simply because you want to improve yourself and gain a new skill. A PDP is useful for most situations where growth, improvement, or development is the aim. Think of it as a plan to organize action!

If you want to achieve your long-term goals, then you need to create short-term goals to serve as milestones or steppingstones to progress. You cannot decide to run a marathon and sign up, hoping for the best.

There are a lot of steps between the decision and the reality. A lot of hard work. The same is true of all goals. Your short-term goals should essentially be the long-term goal broken down into easy steps with constant improvement in mind.

If your goal is to change careers, then you need milestones that revolve around learning and development. You need to take courses, enroll in relevant classes if you need qualifications. You might need to study independently, attend workshops, network, study, join a club, or learn a new skill. All of these are opportunities to gain the knowledge and skills that you will need on the journey to achieving your target.

The Benefits of A Personal Development Plan

So, now you have a better idea of what a PDP is, what it involves, and how it functions, what is the point?

There are plenty of benefits to creating and sticking to your own personal development plan.

- A PDP can help you build on your existing skills.

- A PDP can help you build new skills.

- A PDP can help you plan changes in your career.

- A PDP can help you manage a career progression.

- A PDP can push you to learn.

- A PDP can help you measure and track your progress.
- A PDP can assist you in achieving different objectives.
- A PDP can help define a particular path, whether it's an area of study or your career.
- A PDP can give you a realistic goal to aim for.
- A PDP can help you stay motivated.
- A PDP demonstrates enthusiasm, dedication, and a desire to improve.
- It can serve as a written record of all your efforts.

Personal development is an investment in your future.

The Truth About Personal Development

Personal development, self-improvement, growth. Whatever you call it, it is important that you understand it is not something that just happens. It requires guidance and effort. It will not happen overnight. It will not happen automatically.

Sometimes, it is all about being in the right place, at the right time, and in the right mindset to take the opportunity in front of you. It goes further than that, of course. Consistent personal development requires focused deliberate effort.

Why should you sit down and create a personal development plan?

At certain points in your life, you will have opportunities for development. You may be faced with a personal hero who has an opportunity for you.

Or it might be an opportunity to change things up and tackle something completely new and unexpected. You can't rely on opportunities to just come your way, though. While some of it is down to luck, you are more than capable of engineering some luck for yourself. The harder you are prepared to work, the more open you are to opportunity, the luckier you are going to get.

What does that mean?

If you want certain opportunities, then you need to know what skills are required, where yours lie, and how you can improve them in order to meet the necessary requirements for said opportunity. Work on that. As you do you will start to improve and by improving you create a situation more likely to go your way.

For example, you love writing but you don't share that work with anyone. You watch writers "get lucky" and make millions self-publishing. Or get signed by a publishing house. You could "get lucky" too if you were courageous enough to self-publish.

A PDP can help guide you from where you are now to where you want to be. Once you start self-publishing, you can review your PDP and change things up for your next goal – a writing contract. So, you're putting the work in and creating your own luck and it's all due to the guiding light of a PDP.

If you have no idea where you need to improve or what it takes to improve, then you will never be able to work on that. If you do not bother to plan ahead to work on those skills or outline your path, then you're going to be adrift forever.

Why should you plan personal development and create a written document? Only you can decide what to achieve, what you'd like to achieve, and figure out how best to do that. The power and control are in your hands. They always have been.

But there is a good chance you have not used them effectively up until this point and a personal development plan is the best way for you to do so moving forward. Before you chase your goals, you must know what you need to achieve them. That is an incredibly important part of the process.

As important as it is to plan your career or study, a personal development plan may also be useful in your personal life.

Why You Don't Need A Personal Development Plan

There may be situations where you feel like you need a PDP, but you do not. For example, you may reach a point where you make the conscious decision that you do not want to make deliberate personal development progress. In these cases, it is not a case of being done learning. You will continue to learn from the experiences that you go through. Those are the lessons life must teach you.

You may simply decide that you are in a period where you do not need to document the process as you have done thus far and likely will again. Whether you have achieved something big and you do not have any pressing goals to work on or there's something at play. There will be points in your life where you do not need a PDP.

But, when you do want to improve skills, gain new ones, or change things up, a PDP is a necessary part of the process. Planning helps you take the right action to achieve your goals.

The Elements of a Personal Development Plan

We already touched on what should be in a personal development plan, but it is worth discussing in-depth.

Clarity

Where do you want to be? Why do you want to be there? What does it look like? This is the type of clarity you need to be able to describe in your personal development plan. It's useful to think in terms of time. For example, thinking about the next month, the next six months, the next year, the next five years, and so on.

You should always include as much detail as possible when describing your vision, whether it is your career, hobbies, relationships, or where you plan to live. The more detail you include, down to your emotions, the easier it will be for you to keep a tight grip on that vision when motivation is waning.

Understanding

Before you can figure out how best to develop your plan to achieve the vision you described you need an understanding of the skills necessary to get there. What skills will you need to gain in order to achieve your vision? Which skills will you need to strengthen? Are there weaknesses that you can work on to ensure they don't trip you up?

For example, are there certain skills necessary for a certain role you want to ascend to?

Do you want to move abroad for a period and therefore need to learn a new language?

Do you struggle with situation management and there are skills you can develop to help?

Have you heard that you are lacking in a particular skill set and know that developing them will make you more effective or efficient, whether on your own or in a team?

When you focus on developing new or existing skills, it must be because it is linked to a purpose related to your vision. If you do not have this level of clarity and understanding, then you will struggle to achieve your personal development plans. If your focus is on the wrong skills or actions you will never achieve what you want. If you do not have a clear timescale, you may fall behind.

Standards

What is your current standard? How does that measure up to your desired standard? The difference between your current situation and your desired future situation is the gap where all the work must take place. Where you are now versus where you want to be will determine how much work goes into the situation and how long it will take.

For example, your plan is to move abroad exactly one year from today. You need to work on your language skills. However, if you have visited that country previously or already started learning the language, then you might not have as much work to do as someone who has never once spoken the language or attempted to learn it.

The gap for a total novice is far greater than someone with some skills. You have the same timeline, but the level of work necessary varies depending on the existing skill level.

Priorities

As much as you might like to, you cannot handle everything all at once. You might have a dozen long-term goals you are chasing, but you cannot focus on achieving all of them at the same time. It is too much, and it will only result in you achieving nothing. It is easy to be derailed when you overdo it. Therefore, you must learn to prioritize.

How important is this goal?

How essential is this goal?

How soon do I need to achieve this goal?

This should help you identify which goals to focus on first. The others can be slotted in after that, in order of priority.

Details

You know where you are at (Point A), you even know where you want to be (Point B), but how are you going to move from Point A to Point B? That is where the details count. You need a detailed plan or idea about how you move yourself steadily from Point A to Point B.

It is like your vision, you can use timelines to break it all down to make it clearer, thus easier to create detail. When you have a detailed vision and plan to follow it is much easier to measure progress and stay on track.

The Benefits of Personal Development

We already addressed some of the benefits of creating a personal development man. If that were not enough to sell you on the idea, let us look at the benefits of personal development in general. You are here right now because you are interested in self-improvement and to improve you must invest in yourself and personal development is the investment.

If you are familiar with self-actualization, then you will likely know of Abraham Maslow. Maslow, a psychologist, proposed that all humans have an inherent need for personal development. Self-actualization is the process by which we do so. This is the realization of our talents and potential. This drive is present in all of us. Maslow's theory recognized that how each person develops and grows is dependent on needs. You can only progress to the next need once the preceding level of needs has been addressed.

Thus, the hierarchy of needs was born. At the base of the hierarchy, you will find your basic physiological needs – clothing, food, shelter, oxygen, etc. The next level is safety needs – employment, property, resources, etc. The level above that is love and belonging – family, friends, intimacy, etc. Above that, you will find esteem – recognition, respect, freedom, etc. Finally, at the top, you reach self-actualization – the desire to become everything you possibly can be.

The path you take to get there is your own. Likewise, what some of the details in each level of needs look like will be dependent on your expectations and standards. Your love and belonging needs may look wildly different to your friend because you have different values and priorities. Personal development is a profoundly individual process. It is not a one-size-fits-all situation and it never will be.

- Personal development, as well as a plan, can help you develop your ideas. It is an opportunity to sit down to create ideas, sort, and sift through everything that flutters through your brain.

- Clarity is another benefit that comes from personal development, whether you have created a plan yet or not. No one wants to feel as though they are merely drifting through life without any direction or destination in mind. But that is precisely what so many of us do. We drift through life, complying with societal expectations, and do so with our eyes closed because that is what we thought we were supposed to do. But what do you want? When you start paying attention to your development, you start to gain clarity about your true wants and desires. Your plan will evolve over time and if it does, that means you are doing it right.

- Personal development is empowering! We all need to feel empowered to make decisions and act. Personal development empowers you by helping you recognize talents, weaknesses, and strengths, as well as highlighting how you can appropriately channel them!

- If there is one thing you can expect from life it is that it is going to knock you down from time to time. And personal development is what helps you build the resilience it takes to get back up and try again. It truly does not matter how many times you fail, what matters is that you are willing to keep trying. That is what resilience is.

The ability to take the hit, but not let it keep you down. Personal development, and the plan to match, will help you manage swerves, obstacles, and knocks much more efficiently. It makes the threats seem less threatening and more manageable. An obstacle should not be a game stopper. If you work on personal development, you have a plan, and you build resilience, then an obstacle is a mere game-changer, and you can handle that.

- No one can be truly confident every second of every day, it just is not a natural state of being for humans. That might be because we are chided for being too cocky, that your confidence was stamped out of you and called arrogance, or that someone told you that you were too full of yourself.

If you have a good idea of where you are going and you know how you are going to get there, you have cause to feel confident. You will not feel that way all the time, but with growth and awareness of your skills, confidence will become a much more natural state for you to slip into.

There is another benefit that comes with the confidence that comes with personal development. Others respond well to confidence and it can be inspiring for them.

If you come across as a confident person, it will impact the people around you.

- You do not need me to tell you that you should set goals. You already know it is important. Most of us just do not bother doing it. Or we do. We set a goal in our minds and think about it occasionally, but we don't take any steps to make it happen.

Personal development, and working on a plan, will help you become a much better goal-setter. You will become confident in your ability to structure realistic goals that you can achieve. You will learn how to measure, track, and monitor your progress. And you will pick up skills on how to evaluate, review, and reset goals when circumstances change. As a result, you will become a master at goal-achieving too.

- How you feel about yourself depends on your level of self-esteem. That is not something that matters only now, it matters for the duration of your life. It will influence your progress too. Life naturally dips down and climbs high.

You will always experience a variety of peaks and troughs, in all manner of ways, but particularly in the way you feel about yourself. When you put yourself behind the wheel and become the master of your destiny you will notice more highs in self-esteem than lows. We always feel better about ourselves when we are in control. There is no greater way to take control of your life than with your personal development.

The very act of personal development helps you get to know more about yourself. You learn more about what makes you tick, who you are, what you are, and how you can move forward. Your self-esteem can only grow from here.

- Humans are social creatures and when we build strong relationships, we tend to be happier people. In an ideal world, you would have fantastic friendships, familial connections, and working relationships with your colleagues.

But how often do you find yourself donning a mask to cover up your emotions? You feel the flicker of feelings coming through and you immediately take a breath and steady yourself. While emotional management is an important skill to learn, it is just as important that you take the next step after getting those emotions in check. Which is to open your mouth and constructively express those feelings.

Yes, that is easier said than done, but it must be done. And, personal development, and putting it into a plan, is one of the things that makes that a far simpler prospect. You do not have to push your emotions down and pretend everything is copacetic.

As you invest in yourself through personal development you will start to learn more about yourself, your emotions, and your relationships too. This may result in you letting go of certain relationships, but it is a good thing. Not every person you meet is meant to be in your life forever.

- With personal development, and a plan to boot, you will be teeming with motivation. Having a plan in place that outlines not only where you want to go, but how you will get there, can be a highly motivational tool. It gives you the framework that you need to get to where you want to be. And, if you falter or when you fall, you can review your plan and refocus.

Striking a healthy work-life balance has become an incredibly popular idea in the last decade or so. Once upon a time, our lives were set out in terms of school, work and family, retirement, and death. We now have families later, work longer hours and for more years, and a lot of people will never fully retire. That has changed how we view the importance of enjoying life. A personal development plan can help you ensure that you have plenty of time for living.

- With personal development, comes knowledge. When you plan your future, set your direction, and take off, you will pick up a wide variety of skills, as well as a deeper knowledge of yourself and the world in which you exist.
- With personal development, comes happiness. Why wouldn't you feel happy when you have set your course and have a plan in place to steer on?

Final Thoughts

It can be overwhelming as you start on your journey of self-investment. While it can feel just as overwhelming to sit down and create a personal development plan, it is certainly a tool that will help you on your journey of growth.

There may be times where you feel as though you have no valuable skills or that you know nothing. That is not the case. Of course, you have skills. You have been developing skills your entire life. You have been learning since the day you were born.

While you may feel as though some of your skills are rooted in the job you do now, you would be surprised at just how many transferable skills you possess.

Remember, you do not have to improve everything about yourself all at once. This is a journey, a long one, and today is only the first day. Focus on one or two things at a time and you will not only see improvement as it comes, but you also will not feel as overwhelmed as you expected to. There is not a time limit on this, it is lifelong learning. It is what life is all about.

This is the obligatory page where the author is supposed to lay out his or her credentials and bona fides. But this book is about YOU not me. I have lived a full life and learned from my life's experiences. It is from that life that I share this information so that hopefully you can invest in the most important asset you will ever have- YOU!

CPSIA information can be obtained
at www.ICGtesting.com
Printed in the USA
LVHW012210050821
694387LV00008B/361